POKÉMON™

Ash's Atlas

Written by Shari Last,
Glenn Dakin, and Simon Beecroft

CONTENTS

KALOS REGION 136

ALOLA REGION 162

GALAR REGION 188

ISLAND ADVENTURES 214

Ash Ketchum

Pikachu

Welcome to Ash's world!

This is Ash Ketchum. Ash believes that Pokémon are the most wonderful living creatures! He feels so lucky to share this world with all the different types of Pokémon, from fire-breathing Charizard to sleepy Snorlax, and colorful Hawlucha. They can all be our friends—once we get to know them and learn their ways!

The cool thing about Pokémon is they all have special skills that will blow your mind! They can evolve, so a cute Riolu can become a great Lucario. Best of all, they can become your pal, like Ash's Pikachu. The two go everywhere and do everything together. You can't get better than that!

Ash loves traveling the world, making new friends, and discovering interesting places! With this amazing Atlas you can explore Ash's world too. From his home in the Kanto region, to the sunny islands of the Alola region, or the mythical marvels of the Galar region, there is so much to see!

Ash will be your guide throughout this book. So pack your Poké Ball (to catch Pokémon in) and join him in his travels—as the journey continues!

Charizard

Snorlax

Hawlucha

Lucario

What to Pack

In the Galar region Ash's **Rotom Phone** provides useful data about Pokémon and landmarks. In this book it gives you tips on what to pack when visiting new locations!

KANTO REGION

The Kanto region is known for its bustling cities, its tourist hotspots, and—most of all—its awesome Pokémon tournaments. Trainers flock here to test their skills and to find some of their favorite Pokémon, including Dragonite, Squirtle, and of course, Pikachu!

PALLET TOWN

Ash's hometown is small and sleepy, but it has everything a budding Pokémon Master could need: a kind mom, a safe home, and a world-famous Pokémon professor. The lab belonging to Professor Oak is full of Pokémon, and it is here that Ash starts his journey.

Top Tip!

If you find yourself at the beautiful Xanadu Nursery, watch out! Some of the plants are armed with toxic defenses.

Who's Who?

Ash Ketchum
Ash dreams of becoming a great Pokémon Master. He catches his first Pokémon in Pallet Town and plans to explore the whole Pokémon world.

Delia Ketchum
Ash's mother supports her son completely, even if she does worry about him sometimes.

Professor Samuel Oak
An expert in Pokémon behavior, Professor Oak is a writer and poet, and, of course, the inventor of the Pokédex!

Gary Oak
Professor Oak's grandson always has something to prove. He and Ash are fierce rivals, but they learn to respect one another.

Professor Samuel Oak

Ash Ketchum

TOP 3 MUST SEES

1. Professor Oak's Lab
Visit the lab where the famous Professor Oak carries out his research. You can't miss it—it's the building with the giant windmill!

2. Ash's House
There's no place like home, and nothing as warming as a home-cooked meal.

3. Pokémopolis Ruins
The legend of the ancient city of Pokémopolis has felt a bit more real ever since relics were discovered close to Pallet Town.

FIRST PARTNER POKÉMON

The Kanto region's first partner Pokémon are Bulbasaur, Squirtle, and Charmander. Pikachu also once made an appearance as a first partner Pokémon.

Bulbasaur

Squirtle

Charmander

Pikachu

DID YOU KNOW?

Ash really wanted Squirtle to be his first partner Pokémon. However, Ash overslept and arrived at Professor Oak's Lab late—Pikachu was the only Pokémon left!

VIRIDIAN CITY AND FOREST

A small area with plenty of greenery, Viridian City is fun to explore. The Viridian Gym is one of its grandest buildings, while the modern, domed Pokémon Center is renowned for its excellent Pokémon care.

DID YOU KNOW?

If you see an unusual flying Pokémon—take cover! It's most likely a Meowth-shaped hot-air balloon, which means Team Rocket is on its way.

Who's Who?

Giovanni
Giovanni is the Viridian Gym Leader and boss of Team Rocket, a group of villains who want to steal all the best Pokémon.

Jessie and James
Members of Team Rocket Jessie and James try as hard as they can to complete Giovanni's missions, but somehow always mess things up!

Meowth
The third member of Team Rocket is Meowth. All it wants is to become Giovanni's favorite pet Pokémon.

TOP 3 MUST SEES

1. Pokémon Center
The best place to take your injured Pokémon is the Pokémon Center. It's clean and fully equipped, but is always at risk of an attack by the local villains, Team Rocket.

2. Viridian Gym
Viridian Gym is a gorgeous building with fountains, staircases, and soaring columns. Battles for the Earth Badge are held here, but are often rigged, allowing Trainers to feel the pain of their Pokémon.

3. Viridian Forest
This lush, green space is the perfect escape from the city. It's also the ideal place to spot Bug-type Pokémon, such as Caterpie and Weedle.

SPOT THAT POKÉMON

Viridian City is home to many Bug-type and Flying-type Pokémon, thanks to the nearby Pokémon-friendly habitat, the Viridian Forest. Can you spot Caterpie, Pidgeotto, Weedle, Beedrill, Kakuna, Spearow, Fearow, and Pidgey?

Weedle

Spearow

Caterpie

Jessie

Pidgey

Beedrill

DOS & DON'TS

WITH . . . TEAM ROCKET

Do watch out for them at Viridian Gym—Giovanni, the Gym Leader, is their boss.

Don't trust them! They are always up to no good.

Do whatever you can to stop them from stealing your Pokémon!

James

Don't be surprised when you understand what their Meowth is saying. It is the only known Pokémon that can talk to humans.

Meowth

UNIQUE POKÉMON ENVIRONMENTS

Mount Moon and Dragonite Island are among the most mysterious locations in the Kanto region. Legends and stories about these places are whispered far and wide, from rumors of a meteor with special powers to the question of whether Dragonite Island exists at all.

DID YOU KNOW?

Pieces of Moon Stone are scattered over the ground around Mount Moon. They are very precious and can help Pokémon evolve.

MOUNT MOON

DON'T MISS:
METEOR MYSTERY

- Tall **Mount Moon** towers over the northern Kanto region. Legend says it is the site of an ancient **meteor crash**.

- The meteor is known as the **Moon Stone**. Mount Moon gets its name from this mysterious stone.

SPOT THAT POKÉMON

Some Fairy-type Pokémon live in or around Mount Moon, including Clefairy and Clefable. Swarms of Zubat also fly near the base of the mountain.

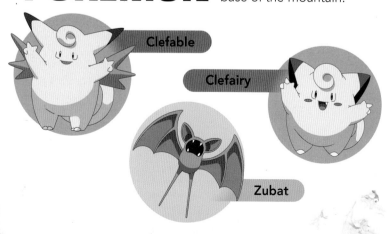

Clefable

Clefairy

Zubat

NEED TO KNOW:
CLEFAIRY

- Clefairy have a **prayer ritual** where they dance around the Moon Stone during a **full moon**.

- It is said **great happiness** will come to those who see the ritual.

- Rumor has it Clefairy come from **outer space**!

DRAGONITE ISLAND

TOP 3 MUST SEES

1. Beautiful Beaches
This island is a tropical paradise, with lots of white sandy beaches to relax on.

2. Waterfall
Visit a waterfall with a hidden cave behind it, where rare Dratini shed their skin.

3. Lush Forests
Dozens of Dragonite sleep in the shade of the island's trees.

TYPICAL WEATHER

The Dragonair create constant storms to keep their island hidden from prying eyes. The storms sometimes wreck passing ships, though local Dragonite will bring survivors to the island to help them recover.

EVOLUTION SOLUTION

Dratini and its evolved form, Dragonair, look similar, but Dragonite looks totally different! One theory is that Dragonite evolved arms to help those shipwrecked by Dragonair's storms.

Dragonite

Dragonair

Dratini

CERULEAN CITY

Trainers flock to this pretty city, which is home to the famous Cerulean Gym. There are lots of great places to hang out after your training is done, including the mall and a gorgeous picnic spot beside the lighthouse.

Misty

What to Pack

A bike—Just in case a flock of Spearow start chasing you and you need to make a quick getaway.

Swimming trunks—For the pool at the Gym.

Your top Water-type Pokémon—They will love battling for the Cascade Badge at the Gym.

A camera—The views from the lighthouse are simply stunning!

Togepi

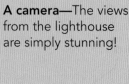
Dewgong

Who's Who?

Misty
The Cerulean Gym Leader Misty loves her Togepi and Water-type Pokémon.

Violet, Lily, and Daisy
Misty's older sisters weren't the best Gym Leaders. They preferred to put on synchronized swimming shows in the Gym's pool instead of organizing battles. Luckily, they decided to hand over leadership to Misty!

TOP 3 MUST SEES

1. Cerulean Gym
A candy-colored Gym with an amazing battlefield pool. Don't miss the aquarium in the basement, which is filled with Water-type Pokémon.

2. Bill's Lighthouse
The tall, white lighthouse stands proudly on a cliff, beaming a color-changing light into the sky to attract Pokémon. Visit the house next door and say hello to Bill, the lighthouse owner and local Pokémon expert.

3. Cerulean Cave
This secret cave is as beautiful as it is mysterious. There are rumors of a powerful Pokémon living in the Cerulean Cave.

SPOT THAT POKÉMON

Plenty of Water-type Pokémon have found a home in the Gym's aquarium, including Goldeen, Horsea, and Starmie. Seel was there too, until it evolved into Dewgong during a battle against Team Rocket.

Seel

Horsea

Starmie

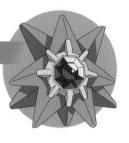

Goldeen

DID YOU KNOW?

There are eight Gyms in the Kanto region and each one offers Trainers a badge if their Pokémon win the battle. If a Trainer wins all eight badges, they can enter the Pokémon League Conference— a tournament Ash can't wait to win!

CITY TOURS

See all the sights in just a few hours on the **Vermilion City** tour bus!

1. The Harbor
The cruise ship *St. Anne* used to dock at the majestic harbor every year until it sank during an attempted Pokémon heist.

2. Cerise Laboratory
This Pokémon research laboratory has a unique design. It has a huge domed park inside called Cerise Park.

3. Vermilion Gym
Daring Trainers visit the Vermilion Gym to compete for the Thunder Badge.

4. Cycling Road
Marvel at the enormous winding bridge that connects Vermilion City with Sunnytown.

TRAINER TIPS

- Lt. Surge is the Vermilion Gym Leader. When he is away training his Electric-type Pokémon, Lt. Surge leaves the Gym in the care of acting Gym Leader Visquez.

- The Vermilion Gym specializes in Electric-type Pokémon like Raichu. They will use some shocking moves in battle. Plan ahead and think about which of your team are best to battle Electric-type Pokémon.

- Lt. Surge will try to confuse you as you enter the Gym. It will be pitch black and then lots of lights will burst into life. Remember to shield your eyes so it's not too bright!

Visquez in battle

Professor Cerise

DID YOU KNOW?

Cerise Park is in the center of the lab building. Ash and Goh keep their Pokémon there when they come to stay.

VERMILION CITY

This charming port city is the perfect place to begin an adventure. Visit the harbor and board a boat to distant islands, or travel by train to exciting new cities. Vermilion City is a place of contrasts, with shining skyscrapers, quaint houses, and Cerise Laboratory that looks like an old castle!

SPOT THAT POKÉMON

Lugia

The Legendary Pokémon Lugia was once spotted in Vermilion City. There are also known to be outbreaks of Ivysaur and Bulbasaur during the famous "Ivysaur March." While this causes traffic, it usually ends with the city's flowers blooming!

Bulbasaur

Ivysaur

Who's Who?

Professor Cerise
This Pokémon expert's lab is in an old building that used to be haunted by the Ghost-type Pokémon Gengar. But Professor Cerise didn't mind!

Chloe
Professor Cerise's daughter is very quiet. She sometimes feels embarrassed when her dad gets too excited about Pokémon!

Goh
Like Ash, Goh has big dreams of catching every Pokémon. He is determined that his first Pokémon will be the Mythical Mew.

Chloe

Goh

KANTO REGION ISLANDS

If you're looking for a top tourist destination, try visiting the Kanto region's beautiful islands. Cinnabar Island is famous for its hot springs and souvenir shops, while Seafoam Island has some of the biggest waves around. Both islands have Pokémon hotspots to keep Trainers happy on their vacation!

CINNABAR ISLAND

NEED TO KNOW: CINNABAR GYM

- Gym Leader **Blaine** is sick of all the tourists. He's closed the old Gym and built a new one inside the volcano. Now only serious Trainers will find it!

- Find the **Gyarados** statue in the hot springs. Use it as a lever to open the volcano.

- Go through the **volcano tunnel** and find a way to open the super-hot door.

? DID YOU KNOW?

The Cinnabar battlefield is inside a volcano, suspended over a sea of lava. The winners of the battle receive the Volcano Badge.

DOS & DON'TS
WITH . . . BLAINE

Do head over to the Big Riddle Inn. It's the starting point if you want to find the Gym.

Don't let Blaine know that you also came here for a bit of surfing.

Do let Blaine know how annoying you think all these tourists are.

Don't be afraid to get a little wet. The path to the Gym is via the hot springs!

SEAFOAM ISLAND

DON'T MISS: SEAFOAM ISLAND

- A huge tidal wave named **Humungadunga** hits the island once every 20 years. Bring your surfboard to try and catch it!

- Nestled among the island's lush greenery is **Professor Westwood V.'s Lab**. Here you will have the chance to learn from one of the Pokédex programmers!

- Visit sunny **Seafoam Beach** for the ultimate place to take a well-earned rest.

What to Pack

Surfboard—A Pikachu named Puka surfed the biggest wave of all time on Seafoam Island!

Sunscreen—Make sure you protect your Pokémon's skin, and your own, when sunbathing.

Fishing rod—To catch fish alongside a Slowpoke.

Puka surfing Humungadunga

SPOT THAT POKÉMON

There are plenty of Water-type Pokémon on Seafoam Island, including Krabby, Magikarp, and the Water- and Psychic-type Pokémon, Slowpoke. You can also spot groups of Gyarados off the coast.

Magikarp

Slowpoke

Krabby

LAVENDER TOWN AND ROCK TUNNEL

A small town in the northeastern Kanto region, Lavender Town is quiet compared to the nearby Saffron City. It's home to the famous Pokémon Tower, which makes it a top destination for Trainers looking to catch a Ghost-type Pokémon for their battle at Saffron Gym.

DID YOU KNOW?

The Battle Dome facility in the area gets a lot of media attention, thanks to the Dome Ace Tucker, a famous actor and Trainer. Challengers will face Tucker in a Double Battle.

TOP 3 MUST SEES

1. Pokémon Tower
The Pokémon Tower is the perfect place to catch some Ghost-type Pokémon— if you dare!

2. Saffron City
The Kanto region's largest metropolis is just outside Lavender Town. Head to Saffron City if you want to experience the hustle and bustle of city life.

3. Rock Tunnel
This pitch-black underground tunnel is a top spot for Trainers to explore and train. Just make sure you bring a light!

DOS & DON'TS
WITH . . . GEODUDE

Do compliment Geodude on its strong, sturdy body when you meet it in the Rock Tunnel.

Don't throw Geodude like a ball—it is extremely heavy!

Do walk carefully when searching for Geodude. The Pokémon gets very angry if you step on it.

Don't bother using Flying-type attacks on Geodude; they are weak against Rock-type Pokémon.

SPOT THAT POKÉMON

Ghost-type Pokémon aplenty can be found in Lavender Town's spooky Pokémon Tower, like Haunter, Gastly, and Gengar. Meanwhile, over at the Rock Tunnel, keep an eye out for Geodude and Tauros.

Gastly

Gengar

Haunter

Tauros

TRAINER TIPS

- The Saffron Gym Leader, Sabrina, looks harmless, but she's actually got incredible telekinetic powers and a fierce temper. Beware!

- Use your Ghost-type Pokémon to battle Sabrina. They are the only ones who will have an advantage over Sabrina's Psychic-type Pokémon, Kadabra.

- Don't lose! Rumor has it Sabrina turns defeated opponents into dolls.

Sabrina with her doll

NEED TO KNOW:
BROCK

- This Gym Leader is also a **talented Pokémon breeder**. He prefers caring for Pokémon to training them.

- He has **nine brothers and sisters**, and he grew up looking after them.

- Brock is an **awesome cook**! His friends and Pokémon always look forward to his meals.

- He has a strong relationship with his Pokémon, **Geodude**.

REVIEW:
PEWTER MUSEUM OF SCIENCE

This famous museum does not disappoint. We saw two floors of incredible Pokémon history and artifacts, including a Fossil Restoration Machine and the revived fossils of Aerodactyl and Kabutops—wow! I loved the digging site where you can dig for your very own fossils.

Who has been the Pewter Gym Leader?

Brock
Brock was the strong, proud Gym Leader of the rock-built Gym.

Flint
Brock's dad takes over as Leader when Brock goes traveling.

Lola
Brock's mom redecorates the Gym as a Water-type Pokémon arena, much to his disgust.

Forrest
Brock's brother, Forrest, is the current Leader.

Brock

Top Tip!

Battle fairly at Pewter Gym. Brock, the Gym Leader, is honorable. He has been known to stop a battle for fear of injuring his opponent's Pokémon.

PEWTER CITY

A city of stone skyscrapers, Pewter City is the destination for Trainers when they are ready to battle for the Boulder Badge. Pewter City is also famous for its Museum of Science, where Pokémon lovers can see rare Fossil Pokémon.

SPOT THAT POKÉMON

Rock-type Pokémon, such as Onix, can be spotted taking on challengers at the Pewter Gym. Also, rare Fossil Pokémon have been revived at the Museum of Science, where they live in the biodome.

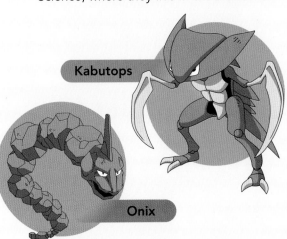

Kabutops

Onix

Aerodactyl

What to Pack

Electric-type Pokémon—Who will enjoy a power boost at the hydroelectric plant.

Top Water-type Pokémon—To give you the biggest advantage in battle against Rock-type Pokémon at the Pewter Gym.

An appetite—You will want to eat as much of Brock's cooking as you can!

Brock cooking for a crowd

PRESERVATION AREA AND HIDDEN VILLAGE

If you want to watch your favorite Pokémon in a relaxing environment, here are two of the region's top spots. The Hidden Village is a secret refuge for Pokémon in need, and the Pokémon Preservation Area is a protected Pokémon reserve, where hundreds of creatures live in their natural habitats.

What to Pack

Binoculars—Spot rare Pokémon hiding in the Pokémon Preservation Area.

Pokédex—So you can learn as much as possible about all the Pokémon you see.

Safari Ball—A Poké Ball that can only be used in the Safari Zone near the Preservation Area.

TOP 3 MUST SEES

1. Laramie Ranch
A Pokémon reserve near the Preservation Area, where Pokémon live in peace. You cannot catch Pokémon here.

2. Laramie Village
The village is situated on the grounds of the ranch. It is where the party for the Big P Pokémon Race is held.

3. The Pokémon Preservation Area
A huge area of forests and plains, where lots of rare, wild Pokémon roam free. Don't try to catch Pokémon here or you will have to answer to Ranger Jenny.

Who's Who?

Melanie

Melanie has built a safe place for injured or abandoned Pokémon, known as the Hidden Village. Here she looks after the Pokémon until they are ready to leave.

Bulbasaur

This Pokémon has volunteered to protect the Hidden Village, but is it doing its job too well? If the Pokémon feel too safe, they won't ever want to leave!

Oddish

A cute Grass- and Poison-type Pokémon, Oddish often finds itself in trouble, but it can always rely on Bulbasaur to rescue it.

Melanie

Bulbasaur

DOS & DON'TS
WITH . . . BULBASAUR

Do make sure the bulb on Bulbasaur's back has space to grow.

Don't send your Pokémon against a Bulbasaur with a Sleep Powder attack, in case Bulbasaur blows it right back at you!

Do watch out for Bulbasaur's vines—they can come out of nowhere!

Don't expect Bulbasaur to be your friend straight away. It needs to learn to trust you first.

SPOT THAT POKÉMON

The Hidden Village is home to Pokémon of all types, such as Rattata and Staryu. In the Pokémon Preservation Area you can observe Sandlash, Nidorina, Dodrio, Kangaskhan, and more!

Kangaskhan

Sandslash

Rattata

Staryu

Nidorina

DID YOU KNOW?

While Trainers enjoy relaxing and watching their Pokémon in their natural habitats, they can't resist a race! The Big P Pokémon Race is an obstacle course across the grounds of the Laramie Ranch. The winner becomes an honorary member of the Laramie clan.

TRAINER TIPS

- The Battle Frontier is a tournament for the best Trainers, who are awarded seven Frontier Symbols.

- Only Trainers who receive the first six Symbols are told the location of the final Battle Frontier facility.

- The final battle for the Brave Symbol is an epic four-on-four match against Pyramid King Brandon, who designed the Battle Pyramid himself.

SPOT THAT POKÉMON

Fennel Valley is home to many Pokémon, including Diglett, Electrode, Gloom, Fearow, and Carvanha. Even a rare Regice has been caught here.

Gloom

Regice

DID YOU KNOW?

The Indigo Plateau also hosts the Kanto Grand Festival. Here, Pokémon Coordinators who hold five Contest Ribbons can compete for the Ribbon Cup and the title of Top Coordinator.

Top Tip!

Practice fishing for Magikarp. In the later rounds of the Indigo Plateau Conference, the competitors are chosen by catching a Magikarp with a letter and number.

NEED TO KNOW: INDIGO PLATEAU CONFERENCE

- Trainers who have won all eight Kanto badges can compete in the **Indigo Plateau Conference**, one of the most prestigious tournaments in the region.

- The Conference starts with four **elimination rounds** in the outer stadiums, before the **final 16 Trainers** compete in the main Indigo Stadium.

- The prize is a **grand trophy** for the winner and **commemorative badges** for everyone who competed.

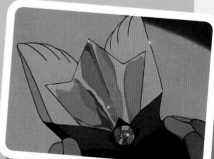

Pokémon League badge

FENNEL VALLEY AND INDIGO PLATEAU

Pokémon battles really draw a crowd, so it's no wonder the stadiums are built to impress. Fennel Valley's Battle Pyramid is the perfect stage for the final Battle Frontier contest. And there couldn't be a better setting for the Indigo League Conference than Indigo Plateau's huge, modern stadium.

Diglett

Electrode

Fearow

1

2

3

TOP 3 MUST SEES

1. Battle Pyramid
The design of this battle facility is a sight to see! Just wait until the battle begins: the roof opens up so there is no ceiling above the battlefield. The sky is the limit.

2. Local Ruins
These are the ruins of Pokélantis, an ancient city ruled by a fearsome king. It is said that the king's spirit is now trapped in a stone orb hidden inside his tomb.

3. Pokémon Center
This is a Pokémon Center like no other: it has a fitness center, hot springs, battlefields, and even its own Contest Hall!

LEGENDARY AND MYTHICAL

The Kanto region is home to some amazing Legendary and Mythical Pokémon, including the three Legendary Birds of Kanto, a mysterious man-made Pokémon, and a friendly Pokémon who might just be the most powerful of all.

Articuno

Type: Ice-Flying
Height: 5 ft 7 in (1.7 m)
The Legendary Freeze Pokémon can bring a chill to the air and cause snow to fall.

Moltres

Type: Fire-Flying
Height: 6 ft 7 in (2 m)
The Legendary Flame Pokémon controls fire and heals itself in the lava of active volcanoes.

Zapdos

Type: Electric-Flying
Height: 5 ft 3 in (1.6 m)

This Legendary Electric Pokémon controls electricity. When it is struck by a bolt of lightning, its power increases.

DID YOU KNOW?

Articuno, Moltres, and Zapdos are known as the three Legendary Birds of Kanto.

Mew

Type: Psychic
Height: 1 ft 4 in (0.4 m)

This Mythical New Species Pokémon can be found in the Kanto region—though it might be tricky to see because it can become invisible!

DID YOU KNOW?

Mew can transform into any Pokémon. Some believe that Mew is the most powerful Pokémon of all.

Mewtwo

Type: Psychic
Height: 6 ft 7 in (2 m)

This Legendary Genetic Pokémon was created by scientists so they could study it. No wonder it's not happy.

DID YOU KNOW?

Mewtwo protects Pokémon who have been mistreated by humans. Ash and his friend Goh once battled Mewtwo on a remote island and were defeated by the strong Pokémon.

ASH'S KANTO REGION TOP 3s

Ash might be from the Kanto region, but he still discovers lots of amazing new sights as he travels across it. Here are some of his Kanto region top threes.

TOP 3 GYMS

1. Cinnabar Gym
It has an awesome lava battlefield.

2. Cerulean Gym
For its battlefield pool and Pokémon-filled aquarium.

3. Viridian Gym
For its beautiful, grand building. (But that's not to say the Gym Leader is grand in the slightest!)

TOP 3 FOODS

1. Brock's rice balls
The best in all of the Kanto region (and maybe the world!)

2. Mom's dinners
Her home-cooked meals are delicious.

3. Ketchup
Okay, this is actually Pikachu's favorite food, but it had to make the list!

TOP 3 POKÉMON HOTSPOTS

1. Pokémon Preservation Area
You've never seen so many wild Pokémon in their natural habitat!

2. Pewter Museum of Science
To see rare Fossil Pokémon.

3. Mount Moon
For a glimpse of Clefairy.

TOP 3 DANGERS

1. Team Rocket
This trio will stop at nothing to kidnap Pokémon.

2. Spooky Ghost-type Pokémon
Lavender Town Pokémon Tower is teeming with these pranksters.

3. Mewtwo
This powerful Pokémon is very tough in battle.

TOP 3 SCENIC SPOTS

1. Bill's Lighthouse
The views are dreamy.

2. The waterfall on Dragonite Island
Perfect for a picnic.

3. The beach on Seafoam Island
Soft sand and plenty of surfing to enjoy.

TOP 3 MYSTERIES

1. What is hidden in the caves of Mount Moon?
The legendary Moon Stone—and lots of Clefairy!

2. Which ancient city has ruins near the Fennel Valley?
The City of Pokélantis.

3. Where is the Cinnabar Gym?
Inside the island's volcano.

JOHTO REGION

Trainers come to this region to explore its many environments, from forests to nature reserves, and to discover its ancient Pokémon folklore. The Johto region boasts big cities, unique Pokémon habitats, and a calendar full of Pokémon festivals!

NEW BARK TOWN

Nestled in a leafy forest, New Bark Town is a quiet, pleasant place and the first stop for Pokémon Trainers as they arrive in the Johto region. Here you can get your first partner Pokémon, sign up for the Johto League, and—of course—watch the Electabuzz baseball team in action.

What to Pack

Electabuzz merchandise— You've got to show your support for the local baseball team.

A Donphan—To sniff out any precious amberite in nearby Amberite Valley.

Pokémon Eggs or any other unusual Pokémon items— To give to Professor Elm!

Donphan

TOP 3 MUST SEES

1. Elm Laboratory
Elm Laboratory is one of the biggest labs you'll ever see. New Trainers can pick their first partner Pokémon here, and experienced Trainers can ask Professor Elm about his research into unusual Pokémon abilities.

2. Pokémon Center
Head to the Pokémon Center to sign up for the Johto League with Nurse Joy. Then plan which Gym you'll head to for your first battle.

3. Wild Pokémon of the Leafy Forest
Just outside New Bark Town is a forest where you can see wild Heracross and Butterfree, as well as an unfriendly colony of Pinsir.

FIRST PARTNER POKÉMON

The Johto region's first partner Pokémon are Chikorita, Cyndaquil, and Totodile. If you hang out at Professor Elm's Lab, you will get to see all sorts of unusual Pokémon, including a Larvitar, who Professor Elm hatched from an Egg.

Larvitar

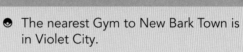

Cyndaquil

Totodile

Chikorita

TRAINER TIPS

- The nearest Gym to New Bark Town is in Violet City.

- To get to Violet City, head out through the forest, past Amberite Valley and Florando.

- Watch out for Haunter and Gengar who like to confuse travelers in the Forest of Illusions. Find the twin sisters Hagatha and Nagatha, who will lend you their Hoothoot to help you find your way through.

Hagatha and Hoothoot

DOS & DON'TS
WITH . . . PROFESSOR ELM

Do ask him about his latest research—it will make him very happy!

Don't say you agree with Professor Oak more than with Professor Elm —the two have quite the rivalry!

Do bring him an Egg from the Pokémon Marine Conservatory. Who knows what it might hatch into?

Don't make a mess in his spotless lab!

VIOLET CITY

Violet City has lots to see and do for Pokémon fans, from battling for the Zephyr Badge to exploring the swaying Sprout Tower. Just watch out for young Pokémon students who go to the local academy—they can get a bit overexcited when they meet new Pokémon!

Top Tip!

Gym Leader Falkner only uses Flying-type Pokémon. Bring your best Electric-type Pokémon for an advantage in battle.

DID YOU KNOW?

There's a secret tunnel path that goes from Violet City through a mountain and leads to a small town on the other side. The tunnel was actually created when one of Team Rocket's plans went wrong!

Who's Who?

Falkner
The Violet Gym Leader is obsessed with flying, so he only uses Flying-type Pokémon in battle.

Earl Dervish
The principal of the Pokémon Academy loves to dance. He juggles being principle with being a dance instructor.

Miss Priscilla
A passionate teacher at the Pokémon Academy, Miss Priscilla teaches young children to train and respect Pokémon.

Falkner

Miss Priscilla

Earl Dervish

TOP 3 MUST SEES

1. Violet City Gym
The Violet Gym is violet, all right! It's a purple spiral tower that leads up to a rooftop battle arena, where Trainers can compete for the Zephyr Badge.

2. Sprout Tower
This super-tall tower is famous for its flexible central beam, which allows the building to sway from side to side. Some say the beam is from a giant Bellsprout.

3. Pokémon Academy
A school for young children who want to be Pokémon Trainers. The teachers at the academy welcome visitors and are eager to introduce the children to new Pokémon.

SPOT THAT POKÉMON!

Falkner uses his beloved Flying-type Pokémon in battle. They include Hoothoot, Dodrio, and Pidgeot. You might also spot Bellsprout near Sprout Tower, and maybe even a wild Sentret.

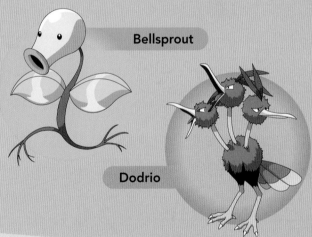

Bellsprout

Dodrio

DID YOU KNOW?

The Pokémon Center can be found in a suburb of Violet City named Happy Town. Nurse Joy has an unusual assistant: Blissey, the Happiness Pokémon, who is perfect at the job.

Blissey

UNIQUE POKÉMON ENVIRONMENTS

Pokémon Trainers travel from far and wide to explore the Johto region's unique Pokémon habitats. From Charizard training grounds to Quagsire celebrations, there's no shortage of places to learn more about Pokémon.

CHARICIFIC VALLEY

The Charicific Valley Nature Reserve is the ultimate training ground for Charizard. It is off-limits to tourists! Trainers can drop off their Charizard here to learn new attacks.

DID YOU KNOW?

Charicific Valley is hard to reach. You'll know you're in the right place when you see the huge stone Charizard statues that mark its entrance.

Liza

Charla

Who's Who?

Liza
There is only one known human living in the Charicific Valley—Liza. She protects the valley and trains the wild Charizard there.

Charla
This pink-bowed Charizard is Liza's trusted Pokémon. Charla becomes good friends with Ash's Charizard when it trains in the valley.

WOOPER POND

Wooper fans won't want to miss Wooper Pond. It's the perfect environment for the Pokémon. There are so many Wooper here that a woman named Olesia set up a day care for them!

NEED TO KNOW:
WOOPER

- Wooper is the **pre-evolutionary** form of Quagsire.

- This Pokémon lives in **cold water** and searches for food when it gets cold outside.

- When walking on land, Wooper covers its body in a **poisonous film** to keep its skin from dehydrating.

Wooper

CHERRYGROVE CITY

Cherrygrove City is the top spot if you're looking for Quagsire. You can't battle or catch them in the city though—they are protected by the local residents. They help find clean water for the city.

DID YOU KNOW?

If you want to see something really special, head to Blue Moon Falls for the yearly Quagsire ritual. Quagsire throw round objects over the waterfall to bring the locals good luck.

Quagsire

GOLDENROD CITY

Goldenrod City is a huge metropolis—the largest in the Johto region, and one of the biggest in the whole Pokémon world! It's easy to get lost here, but Trainers flock to the city anyway. They mainly visit for the Gym, but also to explore some of the best shops in the region.

DID YOU KNOW?

In Goldenrod City, an underground path leads to a shopping arcade. There you will find a shop run by two brothers. They can cut your Pokémon's hair to give them a new look!

TOP 3 MUST SEES

1. Goldenrod Gym
The Gym is a large, impressive building topped with a big, red dome. The arena has space for hundreds of spectators to watch as Trainers battle Gym Leader Whitney for the Plain Badge.

2. Radio Tower
This huge tower in the middle of the city is where DJ Mary broadcasts everyone's favorite radio show, Poké Radio.

3. Goldenrod Galleria
One of the largest buildings in the city, the Galleria is home to all sorts of shops. It is known as the best place to find specialist Pokémon training gear.

CITY TOURS

There are lots of interesting places to visit in and around Goldenrod City. Join this tour and take in some of the highlights.

1. Miltank Dairy
Run by Milton, Whitney's uncle, this dairy farm is a great place to visit if you want to learn more about the Pokémon Miltank.

2. Shopping Arcade
This enormous underground shopping arcade is full of stores, restaurants, and cafés. It's easy to get lost here, but at least you'll have plenty to do while you find your way!

3. Len Town
Just outside Goldenrod City is this small town surrounded by woods full of Ghost-type Pokémon. The locals keep Psychic-type Pokémon with them at all times for protection. You might even spot a Girafarig!

Top Tip!

The forest near Len Town is fascinating to visit. But avoid at all costs if it's Ursaring breeding season—breeding Ursaring are not friendly at all!

NEED TO KNOW: WHITNEY

- Whitney might get lost in her own city, but don't let that fool you when it comes to Pokémon battles. She is a **top Trainer** and hard to beat!

- Whitney doesn't favor one type of Pokémon in battle. She likes to use all **different types**, including Clefairy, Nidorina, and a Miltank from her uncle's dairy.

- Whitney hangs out at **Miltank Dairy**, so it's a good place to find her if you want to get to know her.

AZALEA TOWN

Trainers visit this small, forested town to battle for the Hive Badge at Azalea Gym. The town is also known for its ancient folklore and nearby forests, which are filled with secret shrines, precious Apricorn trees, and lots of Pokémon.

TYPICAL WEATHER

Azalea Town has long, dry spells that often turn into droughts before a huge downpour of heavy rain. Local legends suggest that the heavy rains are caused by the yawns of Slowpoke.

Rain falling on the Slowpoke Well

TOP 3 MUST SEES

1. Azalea Gym
   Located in a forest, Azalea Gym looks more like a garden than a Gym. It is the perfect habitat for Bug-type Pokémon, which are the favored Pokémon of Gym Leader Bugsy.

2. Slowpoke Well
   You can't miss this huge monument just outside of town. It was built to honor the Slowpoke of Azalea Town.

3. Ilex Forest
   On the outskirts of Azalea Town lies the dense, dark Ilex Forest. It is home to a Pokémon Center for traveling Trainers and their Pokémon, and is the site of a mysterious hidden shrine.

TRAINER TIPS

- The battle arena is dotted with trees. This gives an advantage to Pokémon like Spinarak, who can swing from their webs on the branches.

- Bring your best Fire-type Pokémon to give yourself the advantage over Bugsy's Bug-type Pokémon like Scyther.

- Bugsy always keeps his best Pokémon for the last round of the battle.

Bugsy and Scyther

SPOT THAT POKÉMON

Slowpoke are worshipped here and are allowed to roam free. The trees of Azalea Town are full of various wild Pokémon, including the web-spinning Spinarak. Watch out near the Apricorn trees, though—they are home to protective Pineco who will use Self-Destruct if you harvest too many Apricorns.

Spinarak

Pineco

Slowpoke

DON'T MISS: AZALEA TOWN LOCAL PRODUCE

- Locally grown Apricorns can be used to create **Poké Balls with special qualities**, such as Friend Balls, Fast Balls, or Lure Balls.

- The qualities depend on the **colors of the Apricorns**.

- The trees from Ilex Forest produce **top-quality purifying charcoal**. The fuel is famous around the world for its **cleansing powers**.

White Apricorn

DOS & DON'TS
WITH . . . SLOWPOKE

Do have patience with Slowpoke—even though it can take them a while to respond to you.

Do try wearing a Slowpoke costume. It avoids scaring the Pokémon away.

Don't step on a Slowpoke's tail—you will get in trouble with the people of Azalea Town.

Don't ignore it when a Slowpoke yawns. Grab an umbrella!

DID YOU KNOW?

A tale from 400 years ago tells how a Slowpoke saved the town from a terrible drought with its yawn. That's why the citizens of Azalea Town honor the local Slowpoke.

GREAT LAKES

The Johto region is made up of various ecological environments, including many lakes. Some are important historical sites, while others are rumored to have mystical properties. One of the lakes is so mysterious that no one is sure whether it exists at all!

REMORAID LAKE

History: This is usually an empty lake basin because the river dried up years ago.

Famous for: Every 12 years, dozens of Remoraid create a pillar of ice in the basin. The ice sparkles, bathing the lake in rainbow lights before melting and flowing through the riverbed.

? DID YOU KNOW?

The Jet Pokémon Remoraid create the pillar of ice using their Water Gun and Ice Beam moves.

Remoraid

LAKE LUCID

History: This lake was full of pollution from a nearby factory, but three generations of Nurse Joys worked hard to purify it.

Famous for: The renowned Pokémon Center, which specializes in Water-type Pokémon.

? DID YOU KNOW?

Muk, the Stench Pokémon, usually love dirty water, but the polluted Lake Lucid was too disgusting even for them!

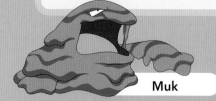

Muk

LAKE RAGE

History: This quiet lake was the location of a Team Rocket base for Project R—a failed attempt to boost Pokémon Evolution using radio waves.

Famous for: Nothing much, just the abandoned Project R building.

LAKE ENLIGHTENMENT

History: A priest once reached enlightenment on the shores of this lake, where he was meditating among the local Slowpoke.

Famous for: Slowpoke Temple, site of the priest's enlightenment and home to a giant golden Slowpoke statue.

ELECTRIC LAKE

History: Legends tell of a sunken temple that houses a crystal charged by the Legendary Pokémon Zapdos.

Famous for: Recharging and healing injured Electric-type Pokémon. But only if you can find the lake in the first place …

DID YOU KNOW?

?

Electric-type Pokémon travel from far and wide to recharge in this legendary lake. Prepare to see Raichu, Electabuzz, Magnemite, Voltorb, and Jolteon.

DID YOU KNOW?

?

Slowpoke lie beside the lake, thinking about the meaning of life while trying to catch Magikarp with their tails. This is why the lake is also known as Lake Slowpoke.

Slowpoke

BLACKTHORN CITY

Blackthorn City is built on legends of the past. It is full of sacred places that honor all Pokémon, but especially Dragon-type Pokémon. Trainers come here to learn from the Gym Leader, Clair, who is an expert in Dragon-type Pokémon.

DID YOU KNOW?

Legend has it that a Dragon-type Pokémon terrorized the city long ago. The first Gym Leader defeated it and kept one of its fangs in memory of the event. The fang rests in Blackthorn City Gym to this day.

SPOT THAT POKÉMON

Blackthorn City is home to thousands of Pokémon, but it's most famous for its Dragon-type Pokémon. Dragonair, Dragonite, and Kingdra can all be found here, as can the Water- and Flying-type Pokémon Gyarados.

Gyarados

Kingdra

TRAINER TIPS

- Gym Leader Clair is caring and kind, but a fierce competitor. She favors Water- and Dragon-type Pokémon.

- The battle arena at Blackthorn City Gym has more than one environment, so be prepared to battle on land, in water, and in the air!

Clair and Dragonair

REVIEW:
DRAGON FANG PURIFICATION RITUAL

Witnessing this sacred ritual was worth the journey! Every three years Gym Leader Clair purifies a fang in water from Blackthorn Lake with a burst of light! I like how the ritual is said to bring happiness to Dragon-type Pokémon—they are my favorite!

TOP 3 MUST SEES

1. Dragon Holy Land
This beautiful meadow is a sanctuary for thousands of Pokémon. The flowers here are always in bloom, and the Pokémon are very happy.

2. Dragon Shrine
This shrine at the edge of Blackthorn Lake houses the Prayer Flame. This celebrates humans and Pokémon living together in peace, and has been burning for 500 years!

3. Dragon's Den
A maze of underground tunnels that connect Dragon Holy Land and Blackthorn Lake. These tunnels were made by ancient dragons.

Dragonite

DOS & DON'TS
WITH . . . DRAGONITE

Do respect the grounds of Dragon Holy Land.

Don't steal the sacred Prayer Flame from the Dragon Shrine—Dragonite will become very angry.

Do remember that although Dragonite is calm and friendly, its wrath can be fiery!

Don't reflect Dragonite's Hyper Beam back at it. It will only end badly for you.

OLIVINE CITY

The Johto region's bustling port city boasts lovely beaches, a cool, modern Gym, and not one but two lighthouses! Trainers come here to win the Mineral Badge, but there is so much more to see in the city, including the impressive Battle Tower.

SPOT THAT POKÉMON

Jasmine favors Steel-type Pokémon for her Gym battles, including Magnemite and Steelix. But her best Pokémon is a helpful Ampharos named Sparkle, who Jasmine doesn't use in battle.

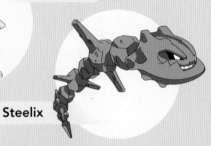

Ampharos

Steelix

Magnemite

Who's Who?

Jasmine
This Gym Leader takes her job very seriously, but she cares for her Pokémon even more seriously. She once cancelled a battle because her Ampharos, Sparkle, was not feeling well.

Janina
Jasmine has several young apprentices at the Gym, including loyal Janina, who can't wait to become a Pokémon Trainer like Jasmine when she's older!

Myron
Jasmine's grandfather Myron is the caretaker of the Shining Lighthouse.

Jasmine

Janina

Myron

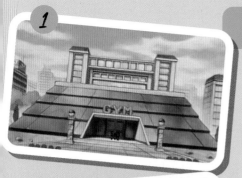

TOP 3 MUST SEES

1. Olivine Gym
Olivine Gym is a modern building, mostly taken up by the battle arena. Trainers head here to compete for the Mineral Badge against Gym Leader Jasmine.

2. Shining Lighthouse
This was the original lighthouse of Olivine City before the new electric one was built. It is known as the Shining Lighthouse because its warning beacon uses light reflected from the tail of Ampharos.

3. Olivine Port
The busy port brings trade and tourists to Olivine City. A ship sails from here to Vermilion City—one of the few ways to travel to and from the Kanto region.

Top Tip!

If you want to enter the tall, glass-covered Battle Tower, you'll need to show your Gym badges to the security guards.

CITY TOURS

Take a break from Olivine City's lighthouses and Gym to explore other nearby sights.

1. Battle Tower
Visit the region's best battle facility near Olivine City.

2. Snowtop Mountain
Between Olivine City and Ecruteak City lies Snowtop Mountain. It is said you can find the Legendary Pokémon Articuno here.

3. Whitestone
Whitestone is a small town just outside the city, where all the buildings are painted white. It's a pretty place to explore in the sunshine.

SILVER TOWN AND MOUNT SILVER

Silver Town is the ultimate destination for Trainers in the Johto region because it's where the Silver Conference is held. Trainers with all eight Johto badges make their way to the town, which lies at the base of Mount Silver.

NEED TO KNOW: SILVER TOWN

- This small town only has around **30 full-time residents**.

- It gets super busy during the **Silver Conference**. Pokémon fans flock to the area in droves.

- Trainers competing in the tournament enjoy luxurious rooms in the **Athlete's Village**, which is near the enormous Silver Stadium.

Silver Stadium

What to Pack

Your eight Johto badges —To compete at the Silver Conference.

A Blaziken—If you have one! To help get rid of the pesky Sneasel!

Your camera— To catch all the exciting Silver Conference action.

Blaziken

DID YOU KNOW?

The Silver Town Pokémon Center is one of the largest in the whole world.

TOP 3 MUST SEES

1. Ho-Oh Shrine
This famous shrine on Mount Silver honors the Rainbow Pokémon, Ho-Oh, who stopped a war hundreds of years ago. A Sacred Flame has been burning inside the shrine ever since.

2. Pokémon Preservation Center
Mount Silver is home to a huge Pokémon preserve. It is protected by Ranger Mason and her colleagues, who are based in the Pokémon Preservation Center.

3. Slowking Mural
Not far from Mount Silver is an ancient Slowking mural that was discovered after an earthquake. It tells how Slowking can evolve from Slowpoke with the help of a King's Rock.

SPOT THAT POKÉMON

Mount Silver is home to a pack of wild Sneasel, who often cause trouble for explorers. The surrounding areas are known for unusual Pokémon sightings, including the rare Evolution of a Slowpoke into a Slowking and an Unown dropping in from the Unown Dimension.

Slowking

Sneasel

Unown

LEGENDARY AND MYTHICAL

Locals love sharing the folklore about the Legendary and Mythical Pokémon of their region. The Johto region's rare Pokémon include one that hides to keep people safe from its immense powers, and one so mysterious that it hasn't been seen for hundreds of years!

Ho-Oh

Type: Fire-Flying
Height: 12 ft 6 in (3.8 m)
The Legendary Rainbow Pokémon is the guardian of the sky. It is said that joy will come to whoever holds one of Ho-Oh's dazzling feathers.

? DID YOU KNOW?

It is said that the Pokémon Ho-Oh has existed since ancient times.

Suicune

Type: Water
Height: 6 ft 7 in (2 m)
The Legendary Aurora Pokémon can clear pollution from rivers and lakes, making the waters pure again.

Entei

Type: Fire
Height: 6 ft 11 in (2.1 m)
The Legendary Volcano Pokémon is said to have come from a volcanic eruption.

Raikou

Type: Electric
Height: 6 ft 3 in (1.9 m)

The Legendary Thunder Pokémon moves at the speed of lightning and roars with the force of thunder.

Lugia

Type: Psychic-Flying
Height: 17 ft 1 in (5.2 m)

The Legendary Diving Pokémon is so huge and powerful that it lives at the bottom of the sea for everyone's safety.

Celebi

Type: Psychic-Grass
Height: 2 ft (0.6 m)

The Mythical Time-Travel Pokémon has come to this world from the future. Seeing Celebi is a very good sign!

WHIRL ISLANDS

The Whirl Islands are a group of beautiful islands surrounded by whirlpools. Most famous for hosting the Whirl Cup, the Whirl Islands also offer many sightseeing opportunities. Visitors can explore rare Pokémon habitats, enjoy island-hopping adventures, and witness ancient local traditions.

BLUE POINT ISLE

Blue Point Isle is named for the great blue rock that helped ancient travelers navigate here. It's the first stop for visitors to the Whirl Islands. You can sign up here for the Whirl Cup. The port town on Blue Point Isle is called Bluefinland. You can get a boat from here to the Yellow Rock Isle.

BOAT TOURS

Hop on a boat for a fun ride to see other nearby islands, but watch out for the whirlpools!

1. Blue Lagoon
Jump on the ferry from Blue Point Isle to visit an ancient Chinchou nesting site.

2. Pudgy Pidgey Isle
See the colony of unusually large, non-flying Pidgey who live on this official Pidgey reserve.

DID YOU KNOW?

Just-hatched Chinchou make their way from the Blue Lagoon on the Blue Isle to the sea. Crowds line the path and throw water on them to keep them safe and wet.

Chinchou

YELLOW ROCK ISLE

This isle is named for its bright yellow rocks. The island's streets are famous for being paved with yellow stones. Tourists flock here to see the native Corsola.

TOP 3 MUST SEES

1. Yellow-paved Streets
Take a walk along the unique yellow-paved streets.

2. Yellow Rock Isle Homes
Make sure you take a look at the houses, which are built on Corsola nests.

3. Corsola Art
Can you spot any art on this island? The locals collect horns shed by the Corsola and display them as art!

RED ROCK ISLE

The Red Rock Isle is named for its red rocks. It is home to the world-famous Whirl Cup. This tournament takes place in the Isle's biggest city, Scarlet City.

Mystic Water Pendant

TOP CONTESTS WHIRL CUP

An epic tournament for Water-type Pokémon Trainers that takes place every three years. The winner receives the title Water Pokémon Alpha Omega and is awarded a Mystic Water Pendant.

SNAPSHOTS FROM THE JOHTO REGION

The Johto region is a place for going on exciting adventures and catching amazing Pokémon. It's also home to many unique festivals and celebrations. It's the perfect place to make memories.

Florando Pokémon Exhibition

A couple of Bellossom belonging to Trainer Bailey compete at the Florando Pokémon Exhibition. Ash's Pikachu shows off a few moves on the big stage too!

Sunflora Festival

Mary, a young Trainer, prepares her Pokémon for its first ever Mareep Festival. Mary's Mareep has wool full of electricity and it does well in the festival.

Team Rocket tries to win a year's supply of instant noodles by entering Meowth (disguised as a Sunflora) in the Sunflora Festival. Unfortunately, things don't go to plan, and there are no free noodles for the team.

Mareep Festival

Palmpona Swap Meet

The Wobbuffet Festival is full of games, food, and fireworks. Battling during the festival isn't allowed, as Wobbuffet never attack first.

Ash's Tauros defeats the champion in the Tauros Run at the Palmpona Swap Meet. Many Trainers try to trade their Pokémon for the Tauros, but Ash doesn't want to give it away.

Wobbuffet Festival

Pokémon Balloon Race

The hot-air balloon contest has lots of balloons shaped like Pokémon. To compete in the race you can use a Flying-type Pokémon to steer the balloon and a Fire-type Pokémon for the hot air.

HOENN REGION

From sunny coastlines to forests bursting with life, the Hoenn region has it all! The land is known for its towering volcano, Mount Chimney, and its collection of unique and fascinating islands.

LITTLEROOT TOWN

Littleroot Town is the first stop for Trainers in the Hoenn region, who can receive their first partner Pokémon here. Most tourists to the region simply pass through on their way to more exciting locations, and some call Littleroot Town "the city whose colors will never change."

Top Tip!

Don't be tempted to explore the mountains around Littleroot Town. A pack of wild Poochyena are very protective of their territory!

FIRST PARTNER POKÉMON

Trainers will get to choose from Mudkip, Torchic, and Treecko as their first partner Pokémon in the Hoenn region. Which one would you pick?

Who's Who?

Professor Birch
This smart professor gives Trainers their first Pokémon— that is, if they can catch up with him. He's so busy with his field research, he's always rushing from one place to the next!

Joshua
Professor Birch's research assistant, Joshua, is used to his mentor's extreme experiments.

Professor Alden
Professor Alden studies the Oldale Ruins, so he is staying at the Oldale Pokémon Center.

Professor Birch

Treecko

Mudkip

Torchic

TOP 3 MUST SEES

1. Professor Birch's Laboratory
This lab is made up of three modest buildings nestled among the trees on the outskirts of the city. Don't be fooled though—this is where Professor Birch conducts wild and often dangerous research!

2. Littleroot Town Port
There's something soothing about watching the boats come and go at the Hoenn region's port. It's also great to see the excitement on Trainers' faces as they reach a new region!

3. Littleroot Beach
See the beautiful migration of the Beautifly. This amazing natural event only occurs once a year, for a very short time during a north wind.

DAY TRIP TO ...
OLDALE TOWN

Oldale Ruins
Wake up early so you have plenty of time to explore the fascinating Oldale Ruins, with its mysterious wall drawings and secret stone chamber that is said to be a portal to the ancient Pokémon world.

Enjoy a delicious picnic
The fields of grass near Oldale Town are perfect for a picnic with friends before returning to Littleroot Town's port and continuing your travels.

SPOT THAT POKÉMON

There's a Relicanth in a hidden underwater pool at the Oldale Ruins. The pool can only be reached during daylight hours.

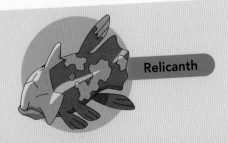

Relicanth

GREAT HOENN REGION CITIES

Trainers will want to find the closest Gym and start collecting those Hoenn badges. Many head straight to quiet Petalburg City to compete for the Balance Badge, before making their way to big, bustling Mauville City to battle for the Dynamo Badge.

Local Celebrity
Petalburg Gym Leader Norman is a celebrity in North Petalburg. You can follow his life in the newspapers and even buy Norman mugs at local stores!

News

PETALBURG CITY

Norman

May

Max

Who's Who?

Norman
Norman is the Petalburg Gym Leader, and father of May and Max. Norman cares for his Pokémon and teaches his children and battle opponents to do the same.

May
May wants to travel the world. She loves finding exciting new places, and—even better—delicious new foods! May becomes a Pokémon Coordinator and sets off to the Johto region to make her dreams a reality.

Max
May's younger brother, Max, wants to be a Pokémon Trainer like his dad. His Pokémon knowledge is nothing short of amazing.

MAUVILLE CITY

Wattson

DOS & DON'TS
WITH . . . WATTSON

Do expect lots of surprises from this fun-loving Gym Leader.

Don't go to Mauville Gym if you hate surprises.

Do head to the abandoned power plant to watch him training.

Don't get a shock when he lets out one of his loud, hearty laughs.

TOP 3 MUST SEES

1. Mauville Gym
This is without a doubt one of the most fun Gyms around, with one of the friendliest Leaders—Wattson. Expect lots of surprises, including a roller coaster and a Raikou robot!

2. Abandoned Power Plant
Take a short trip to an island just off the coast of Mauville City to explore the abandoned power plant and catch the Electric-type Pokémon who live there.

3. Mauville City Beach
This gorgeous, long beach has soft sand and calming ocean waves.

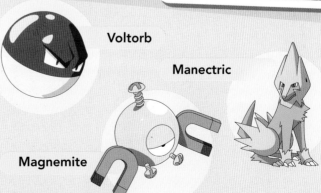

SPOT THAT POKÉMON!

Wattson favors Electric-type Pokémon such as Voltorb and Magnemite. His Manectric evolved from an Electrike after defeating Team Rocket in battle.

Voltorb

Manectric

Magnemite

UNIQUE POKÉMON ENVIRONMENTS

The Hoenn region is home to a lot of varied Pokémon, from cheery Togepi and whiskered Whiscash to hungry Gulpin and grumpy Shroomish. Tourists and Trainers love finding unusual spots to see their favorite Pokémon. Which of these places will you visit first?

Where TOGEPI are worshipped

The residents of the mysterious Mirage Kingdom worship Togepi as the guardians of peace and freedom. Togepi Paradise is a mystical place where Togepi are born. If Mirage Kingdom isn't ruled by someone kind, Togepi Paradise will start to fade.

Where to find it: Mirage Kingdom is across the desert from Mauville City and Lavaridge Town. It is hidden by the mountains.

Togepi

Where GULPIN invade a town

Every year, Gulpin, the Stomach Pokémon, run riot through this small town, eating everything they find. Most people don't even know what the town's real name is. Everyone just calls it Gulpin Town.

Where to find it: Close to Petalburg City.

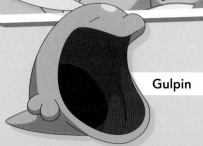

Gulpin

Where a giant WHISCASH evades capture

Nero's Lake is a glorious lake where a giant Whiscash—that has been named Nero—lives. A fisherman has been trying to catch Nero for 50 years, but has never been successful.

Where to find it: Just past the Forbidden Forest, near Fortree City.

Whiscash

Where to see SHROOMISH and BRELOOM in the wild

The Shroomish Forest is so named because of the hundreds of Shroomish living there. Or maybe it's thousands. Visiting the forest can be dangerous as the Shroomish, and its Evolution Breloom, aren't very friendly to visitors. Especially if anyone dares to steal the Pokémon's food!

Where to find it: Just outside Fortree City.

Breloom

Shroomish

Where there are more SLAKOTH than anywhere else!

The Banana Slakoth and Vigoroth Garden is a theme park with many rides and attractions. The biggest attraction is the huge number of Slakoth. And now there's a Vigoroth here too, since one Slakoth evolved.

Where to find it: Near Lilycove City.

Slakoth

Vigoroth

ISLAND-HOPPING

The Hoenn region has loads of small islands, which are perfect for a day of island-hopping. You will see unique environments, historical sites, and plenty of unusual Pokémon. Find a boat and see where the waters take you!

Top Tip!

The Hoenn region is famous for its berries. Before your island adventures, stock up on berries at the Lilycove City Berry Market.

Donto Island

A very small island. Look out for wild Donphan.

Wailmer Island

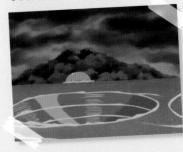

Don't get too close to this isle. It's surrounded by whirlpools.

Bomba Island

Home to the only Battle Judge training school in the world!

Maisie Island

So many Clamperl here! Plus a Clamperl research facility.

A-B-C Islands

Listen to the locals debate who is better: Gorebyss or Huntail.

Muscle Island

Famous training and bodybuilding grounds.

SPOT THAT POKÉMON

Keep your eyes peeled to see wild Wynaut on Mirage Island, native Wailmer on Wailmer Island, hundreds of Clamperl on Maisie Island, and the frequent races between Gorebyss and Huntail Trainers on the A-B-C Islands.

Clamperl

Wynaut

Wailmer

NEED TO KNOW: DRAKE

May

- Drake is a **clipper ship captain** who sails the region's seas.

- He enjoys **hunting for treasure** and has lots of sea knowledge.

What to Pack

Basket to collect berries—There are many berry-picking spots on the islands.

Surfboard—For the famous waves of Dewford Island.

Map—You don't want to get caught in the whirlpools around Wailmer or Mirage Islands!

May's Purple Surprise Pokéblock Recipe

- 2 Pecha Berries
- 1 Oran Berry
- 1 Bluk Berry
- ¼ Tamato Berry

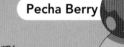

Pecha Berry

Tamato Berry

Oran Berry

IZABE ISLAND

One of the largest islands in the Hoenn region, Izabe Island has several towns and cities, plus some fascinating historical sites. Don't miss Izabe's rather unusual Pokémon reserve and Lake Izabe, with its giant stone Poké Ball!

REVIEW:
LAKE IZABE

◉◉◉◉◉

I loved learning the history behind the giant Poké Ball in the middle of the lake. But apparently, there's an ancient Pokémon inside that once destroyed half the island! I spent the trip nervous someone would let it out again!

TOP 3 MUST SEES

1. Square Top
The highest mountain on Izabe Island, Square Top has a cube-shaped peak. It is also the heart of the local Absol's territory.

2. Trapinch Underground Lake
Huge holes in the rocky desert landscape lead to the Trapinch Underground Labyrinth. There is a lake beneath the Labyrinth where Trapinch can evolve into Vibrava.

3. Valley of Destruction
The valley was destroyed years ago by an ancient force that came out of a stone Poké Ball. You can still see the Poké Ball on a clifftop!

CITY TOURS

After taking in all the natural wonders of the island, take a tour to see its exciting towns and cities.

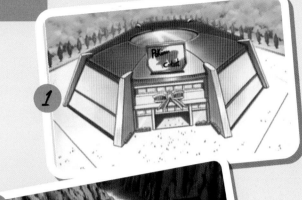

1. Purika City

Visit Izabe's largest city and the home of the Purika City Pokémon Contest.

2. Riyado Town

This small town in the mountains is where wild Absol have been said to warn he locals of upcoming disasters, like flooding.

3. Cerosi Town

Cerosi Town has useful ferry links to nearby Sootopolis City. The surrounding forests are home to Ralts and its Evolutions, Kirlia and Gardevoir.

Top Tip!

Watch out for the wild Snorunt in the mountains around Cerosi Town. They like to steal small items from people passing through.

DID YOU KNOW?

The ancient destructive force is a huge Claydoll. It's 20 times bigger than a regular Claydoll. Something that big is hard to get back into its Poké Ball!

SLATEPORT CITY

Slateport City is home to two great Pokémon tournaments—the Slateport Pokémon Contest and the Hoenn Grand Festival. It also has many tourist attractions, including the port, museums, and plenty of Pokémon!

Top Tip!

If you want to get invited on board the luxurious ocean liner the St. Flower, you'll need to be either a contestant in the Hoenn Grand Festival or the guest of one!

TOP 3 MUST SEES

1. Forsaken Ship
An old cruise ship ran aground years ago just beyond Slateport City. It lay abandoned for years, but it's now been restored into a safe place for any wild Pokémon who are crossing the ocean.

2. Slateport Marine Museum
Water-type Pokémon Trainers love this museum, which is run by Captain Stern, a Pokémon marine biologist. There's lots to see, including a model submarine, water samples from various regions, and a rock from the ocean floor.

3. Misty Village
Just outside of Slateport City, Misty Village is famous for its lighthouse, which uses a special Light Stone—powered by Electric-type Pokémon—to guide ships to safety.

SPOT THAT POKÉMON!

Lots of interesting Pokémon live in the forests around Slateport City, including Nuzleaf and its Evolution, Shiftry, as well as wild Seedot and Oddish. And if you look out into the waters off Slateport City, you might spot a Wailord, one of the largest known Pokémon.

Shiftry

Seedot

Nuzleaf

DID YOU KNOW?

Two Cheering Pokémon, Plusle and Minun, power the Light Stone at the lighthouse in Misty Village.

Minun

Plusle

DOS & DON'TS
WITH . . . PLUSLE AND MINUN

Do keep Plusle and Minun together—it makes them happy!

Don't be surprised if Plusle cries when its teammates lose.

Do encourage them to use their Helping Hand move together.

Don't underestimate them: they might be cute but they can be powerful, too.

SPOT THAT POKÉMON

The mountains around Lavaridge Town are home to wild groups of Spinda. Each Spinda has unique markings. Mount Chimney's famous hot springs were also once frozen by some Glalie protecting a Snorunt.

Glalie

Spinda

Snorunt

GETTING THERE

1. The Jagged Path
This path leads down from Mount Chimney to Lavaridge Town, but it is no easy route.

2. The Fiery Path
There is a shortcut from nearby Fallarbor Town, a tunnel known as the Fiery Path. But watch out for the Slugma who live inside the tunnel. They are fiercely protective of their home!

3. The Valley of Steel
On the other side of Lavaridge Town is the Valley of Steel, and it's very unwelcoming! The Steel-type Pokémon who live there like Steelix, Magnemite, and Skarmory are not friendly at all.

TRAINER TIPS

- You can find Lavaridge Gym next to a canal, just outside the city. Here you can battle for the Heat Badge.

- Don't be surprised if Flannery, the Gym Leader, makes last-minute changes to the battle rules.

- Flannery mainly uses Fire-type Pokémon in battle. Bring your best Water-type Pokémon and Ground-type Pokémon to have a chance of beating them!

Lavaridge Gym

LAVARIDGE TOWN

Lavaridge Town is named for the lava that flows from nearby Mount Chimney. Thanks to the natural volcanic heat from the magma that bubbles underground, the town has famous soothing and healing hot springs.

DON'T MISS: MOUNT CHIMNEY

- The Hoenn region's **most famous landmark**, Mount Chimney towers over the surrounding areas.

- You can catch a **cable car** at its base and travel directly over the smoking volcano. It's an exhilarating ride!

Who's Who?

Flannery
Gym Leader Flannery is as fiery as the molten rock beneath Mount Chimney. She knows she should keep a cool head in battle, but it's a skill she's still trying to master.

Julie
A former Pokémon Coordinator, Julie uses all her knowledge to run a Numel Ranch on the outskirts of the town. She uses her trusty Furret to help round up the slow-moving Numel.

Hodge
Hodge is a friendly Pokémon Trainer from Lavaridge Town. Once, Lavaridge's hot springs dried up and Hodge asked Ash to help figure out what was going on.

Flannery

Julie

Hodge

FORTREE CITY

Almost hidden by the forest, Fortree City is a place you might not even notice! Most of its residents live in treehouses, which are connected by long bridges suspended above the forest floor. You won't miss Fortree Gym though— its high stone walls tower over the surrounding trees.

TOP FESTIVALS

The Feather Carnival
This festival is held every year in the village square. It is a celebration of Flying-type Pokémon, and there are plenty of rides, food stalls, and activities to enjoy.

TRAINER TIPS

- ☻ The entrance to Fortree Gym is halfway up the enormous stone staircase, but the battle arena is on the roof.

- ☻ Gym Leader Winona is a Flying-type Pokémon expert, so bring your Rock, Steel, or Electric-type Pokémon if you want a chance to win the Feather Badge. Better yet, train your top Flying-type Pokémon!

- ☻ Battles begin on top of huge podiums, so make sure you've mastered your fear of heights!

Fortree Gym

SPOT THAT POKÉMON

Gym Leader Winona's favorite Pokémon is a large Skarmory. Winona rides on Skarmory at the end of the Feather Carnival and controls a large formation of Flying-type Pokémon—even though most of them are not her own!

Skarmory

DON'T MISS:
WEATHER INSTITUTE

- This large research facility **collects weather data** from every region in the world.

- The **big satellite dish** can manipulate local weather.

Weather Institute

REVIEW:
EMILY'S HOTEL

ⓐ ⓐ ⓐ ⓐ ⓐ

Loved staying at this mansion hotel on the way to Fortree City. It was the childhood home of the owner, Emily, who has been remodeling it with the help of her Shuppet. Lovely big rooms and a delicious breakfast. Best part is the hidden playroom—my kids loved it!

DID YOU KNOW?

Bart, a researcher at the Weather Institute, has created a Pokémon named Castform. Its appearance changes depending on the weather.

Castform

NEED TO KNOW:
FORBIDDEN FOREST

- Keep out of the **protected forest**, which lies just outside the city.

- The wall was built to **stop Trainers** from coming in and capturing native Grass-type Pokémon.

Forbidden Forest wall

SOOTOPOLIS CITY

Sootopolis City is a beautiful city built on the gentle slopes of the crater of an underwater volcano. It is known as "The Water City", and between its port, Gym, and theater, it really lives up to its reputation!

DON'T MISS:
SOOTOPOLIS THEATER

- The brand new Sootopolis Theater has a **moat around the stage**.

- Expect **incredible performances**, including shows by some of the local Water-type Pokémon and their Trainers.

Who's Who?

Juan
Sootopolis Gym Leader Juan is a Water-type Pokémon expert and former Top Coordinator. His primary Pokémon is Sealeo, a Water- and Ice-type Pokémon.

Sebastian
Juan's assistant at the Gym, Sebastian manages the Gym and tends to its beautiful gardens.

Juan

Sebastian

TRAINER TIPS

- Sootopolis Gym is a beautiful building with arched windows, set in picturesque grounds. Don't let this fool you into thinking the battles will be easy!

- The battles take place in two rounds, using five Pokémon altogether. First is a Double Battle, second is a battle with your remaining Pokémon.

- The battle arena changes for each round. For the first round it's a swimming pool, then it changes to a mixture of water and land for the second round.

Sootopolis Gym

Top Tip!

There's only one way to reach Sootopolis City, and that's by ferry. You can catch one at Cerosi Town.

SPOT THAT POKÉMON

Juan uses various Water-type Pokémon in battle at the Sootopolis Gym, like Milotic, Sealeo, and Seaking.

Seaking

Sealeo

Milotic

DID YOU KNOW?

Trainers with all eight badges head to the Ever Grande Conference in Ever Grande City, an island not far from Sootopolis City. Ever Grande welcomes tourists and fans, with plenty of restaurants and shops.

TASTY FOODS
CHICKEN NOODLES

Delicious chicken noodles can be found in Ever Grande, if you know where to look. Ever Grande Noodle Nosh is one of the best places to eat in the Hoenn region.

HOENN REGION ADVENTURES

Lilycove City is the place where ocean adventures begin! The busy port has ferries to nearly all the islands of the Hoenn region. One of the bigger islands near Lilycove is Mossdeep City, where Trainers go to battle for the Mind Badge.

LILYCOVE CITY

TOP 3 MUST SEES

1. Berry Market
Find the tastiest berries in all of the Hoenn region at this famous market. Enjoy them as a snack or turn them into a Pokéblock.

2. Volley Town
In the mountains outside Lilycove City lies Volley Town, an old-fashioned town that looks like it's from the Wild West.

3. Camerupt Point
This breathtaking spot at the edge of Volley Town is where the mountains give way to the sky and the rock formations look like the humps on a Camerupt's back.

MOSSDEEP CITY

Baltoy

Liza and Tate

Jin

Who's Who?

Liza and Tate
There are two Gym Leaders at Mossdeep Gym: twins Liza and Tate. Liza takes battling very seriously, while her brother Tate just wants her to stop reminding him that she's older than he is!

Jin
Liza and Tate's father, Jin, is the director of the Mossdeep Space Center and an astronaut who researches extraterrestrial Pokémon.

DON'T MISS:
MOSSDEEP CITY SPACE CENTER

- Mossdeep Space Center is the base for many **space missions**, including launching the Sunflora Weather Satellite, Ho-Oh Three, and various space shuttles.

TRAINER TIPS

- Joint Gym Leaders Liza and Tate work together during battle. You will need all your skills to defeat them and their Pokémon, Lunatone and Solrock.

- The battle arena includes the domed roof areas, so you'll be battling on the ground and in the air.

- Be prepared to battle in zero gravity!

Mossdeep Gym

LEGENDARY AND MYTHICAL

The epic rivalry between two of the Hoenn region's Legendary Pokémon, Groudon and Kyogre, is world famous. These two mighty forces channel the powers of land and sea—and they battle continuously. Other Legendary and Mythical Pokémon include Rayquaza, Latios, Latias, and Deoxys.

DID YOU KNOW?

Two orbs were made to control the powers of Groudon and Kyogre—a Blue Orb to control Groudon and a Red Orb to control Kyogre. But the humans who used the orbs grew evil, so the orbs were eventually hidden.

Groudon
Type: Ground
Height: 11 ft 6 in (3.5 m)
The Legendary Continent Pokémon channels the full power of the land.

Kyogre
Type: Water
Height: 14 ft 9 in (4.5 m)
The Legendary Sea Basin Pokémon channels the full power of the seas.

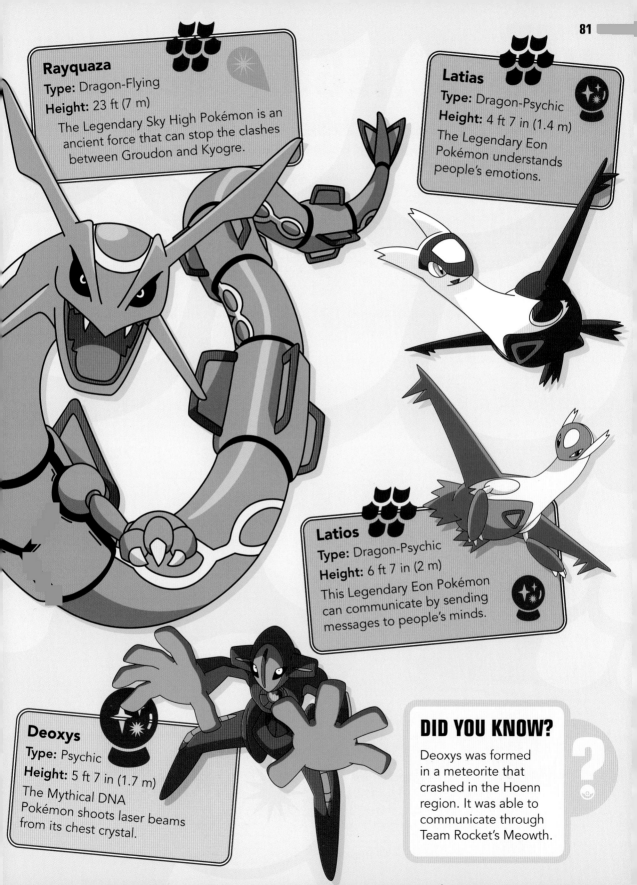

Rayquaza

Type: Dragon-Flying

Height: 23 ft (7 m)

The Legendary Sky High Pokémon is an ancient force that can stop the clashes between Groudon and Kyogre.

Latias

Type: Dragon-Psychic

Height: 4 ft 7 in (1.4 m)

The Legendary Eon Pokémon understands people's emotions.

Latios

Type: Dragon-Psychic

Height: 6 ft 7 in (2 m)

This Legendary Eon Pokémon can communicate by sending messages to people's minds.

Deoxys

Type: Psychic

Height: 5 ft 7 in (1.7 m)

The Mythical DNA Pokémon shoots laser beams from its chest crystal.

DID YOU KNOW?

Deoxys was formed in a meteorite that crashed in the Hoenn region. It was able to communicate through Team Rocket's Meowth.

HuENN REGIuN REVIEW

Exploring the Hoenn region is a Trainer's dream. Wherever Ash's travels take him, its always nice to look back on his top adventures and best experiences.

GYM BATTLES

There are some spectacular Gyms in the Hoenn region, like the super-fun Mauville Gym. They are all challenging, for sure, but the one that sticks out for Ash is Sootopolis Gym, with its changing battle arena. That was tricky, but Ash managed to win the Rain Badge!

FESTIVAL FUN

The Hoenn region has lots of festivals where you can meet the residents, taste local foods, and relax. The best were the Feather Carnival and the May Festival, where Ash got to see Firefly Pokémon Illumise and Volbeat dance at Lake May.

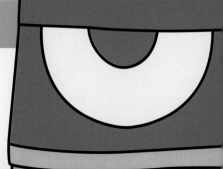

ISLAND ADVENTURES

One of the best trips was the island-hopping adventure. Ash went from Lilycove City across the sea to visit many small, unique islands. Seeing all the Clamperl on Maisie Island was a highlight!

Clamperl

ANCIENT MYSTERIES

There are so many legends and ancient mysteries to discover in the Hoenn region. Ash found the Oldale Ruins fascinating, but he also loved the Baltoy Ruins at the mist-covered Kirikiri Mountain.

POKÉMON SUCCESS

In this region, Ash managed to catch some Pokémon he really wanted like Skitty, Gulpin, Spoink, Ralts, and Wynaut!

Skitty

Spoink

Ralts

THE NOT-SO-GOOD PARTS

The Hoenn region is great, but there are a few people who are not so great. During Ash's travels he was unlucky enough to come across both Team Magma and Team Aqua. Team Magma interrupted his tour of the Oldale Ruins. They were searching for a Blue Orb. And Team Aqua invaded the Weather Institute at Fortree City looking for a Red Orb!

Team Magma

? DID YOU KNOW?

The leader of Team Magma is named Maxie and the leader of Team Aqua is named Archie.

SINNOH REGION

Mountainous and rugged, the Sinnoh region has lots to explore. A snow-topped mountain range runs down the middle of the main island, with many cities, towns, forests, and lakes to discover.

FIRST PARTNER POKÉMON

Twinleaf and Sandgem are great places to find Water-type Pokémon. You can also meet the three first partner Pokémon Turtwig, Chimchar, and Piplup in Professor Rowan's Lab.

Chimchar

Piplup

Turtwig

Ariados

TOP 3 MUST SEES

1. Rowan Research Lab
Professor Rowan's Laboratory is Sandgem Town's landmark. The Professor studies Pokémon here.

2. Lake Verity
This is a secret entrance to another world, where Legendary Pokémon called the Lake Guardians reside.

3. Twinleaf Auditorium
This auditorium has hosted many great speakers. Professor Oak once came to give a lecture on the interrelation of Pokémon and Evolutionary stones.

DOS & DON'TS
WITH . . . ARIADOS

Do avoid the forest outside Sandgem Town— it's full of these Long Leg Pokémon!

Don't pay Ariados a visit at night. That's when they hunt for prey.

Do watch your step. Ariados create sticky webs from threads spewed from their mouths.

Don't get too close! This Pokémon's large fangs can leave a nasty bite.

TWINLEAF TOWN AND SANDGEM TOWN

Twinleaf Town is a gentle, leafy town surrounded by wide open fields. Sandgem Town is situated next to the beach, with a salty scent in the air. Both towns are found on the southern part of the Sinnoh region.

DON'T MISS: TWINLEAF TOWN

- Behind Dawn's house is a **battlefield** where her mom, Johanna, trains junior Coordinators.

- If you are lucky, Xatu may invite you to the mysterious **Xatu's Circus**. This building only appears around the time of the Twinleaf Festival.

TOP FESTIVALS

Twinleaf Festival
This event is held annually in Twinleaf Town. The highlight is a Pokémon tournament called the Festival Battle Challenge.

Who's Who?

Professor Rowan
Sandgem Town's resident Pokémon expert doesn't smile much—but it's only because he's lost in thought.

Dawn
Twinleaf Town is the hometown of 10-year-old Pokémon Coordinator and adventurer Dawn.

Kenny
Dawn's childhood friend Kenny is also a Pokémon Coordinator. He loves to remind Dawn of embarrassing moments from her childhood.

Dawn

Professor Rowan

JUBILIFE CITY

Jubilife City is the biggest city in the Sinnoh region, with many skyscrapers. It was carved out of the side of a mountain! Jubilife City has its own grand Contest Hall where different Pokémon Contests take place.

Top Tip!

Pokétch are must-have items—but beware of fakes!

DON'T MISS:
CITY OUTSKIRTS

- You can walk from Jubilife City to Eterna City through a **beautiful forest**.

- There are lots of sights to see along this route, like **peaceful lakes**, **fields of flowers**, and **fresh springs**.

- Watch out for the **unpredictable weather** and **aggressive Pokémon!**

What to Pack

Contest rule book—Well, you wouldn't want to get a yellow card, would you?

Ribbon case—Perfect for storing and displaying any Ribbons you win.

Ball Capsule and Envelope of Seals —A Ball Capsule attaches to a Poké Ball and adds special effects in battle. Seals create special effects when your Pokémon first appears.

Chloe camping by the lakeside

Ball Capsules and Seals

TOP 3 MUST SEES

1. Jubilife City Contest Hall
During a Pokémon Contest the Contest Hall is busy with contestants and spectators, as well as many food and goods stalls.

2. The Pokétch Company HQ
Pokétch devices are perfect for Pokémon Coordinators to monitor their Pokémon and perform other tasks. The Company is always creating new models with extra features.

3. B-Button League HQ
Visit the HQ of the B-Button League. Members of this unusual organization choose to strengthen and beautify their Pokémon without using Pokémon Evolution.

SPOT THAT POKÉMON

If you visit the B-Button League, you might see Feebas or Magikarp. B-Buttoners prize weaker species like these—they like the challenge of training them!

Feebas

Magikarp

TOP CONTEST:
JUBILIFE CITY POKÉMON CONTEST

Show off your Pokémon's style and skill in the Performance Stage, then see if you can win the Contest Battles. The winner receives the prestigious Jubilife Ribbon!

Jubilife Ribbon

UNIQUE POKÉMON ENVIRONMENTS

Many unusual places can be discovered in between the larger towns and cities in the Sinnoh region—if you know where to look. Huge woods such as Eterna Forest contain hidden secrets such as the awe-inspiring Amber Castle. But watch out for mischievous Pokémon in Bewilder Forest.

BEWILDER FOREST

The Bewilder Forest is full of dangers! There are herds of Stantler—Psychic-type Pokémon that use their glowing antlers to create disorienting mind illusions. There are swarms of Bug- and Poison-type Beedrill armed with poison stingers, and huge, powerful Ursaring chase unwary travelers when they are hungry.

LAKE PSYDUCK

Lake Psyduck is shaped like a Psyduck's foot. The Psyduck who live here often battle the group of Muk who want to take it over.

BIDOOF COLONY

Squeeze through a narrow gap in a cliff by a waterfall and you'll discover a secret colony of Bidoof. They gnaw on logs and rocks—and sometimes people's homes!

AMBER CASTLE

Hidden behind a waterfall in Eterna Forest, Amber Castle is a real gem! It is the home of a large swarm of Combee, who make super-sweet Enchanted Honey.

Vespiquen

DOS & DON'TS

WITH . . . VESPIQUEN

Do address the ruler of the Amber Castle with great respect.

Don't anger Vespiquen—it might use a Power Gem attack on you.

Do thank the Pokémon if it gives you a pot of Enchanted Honey.

Don't battle in the Amber Castle—its walls are very fragile.

KEY POKÉMON

Combee

Psyduck

Steelix

Muk

You can spot many interesting Pokémon in these areas. Combee have hexagonal faces, Psyduck have strong psychic powers, and Muk are made of toxic, living sludge! Rampaging Steelix terrorize Bidoof.

DID YOU KNOW?

Combee can join together to form protective Combee Walls.

OREBURGH CITY

Oreburgh City is known as the City of Energy. This vibrant, active mining town nestles beside a mountain range in the central Sinnoh region. Its key attractions include the famous Oreburgh Mine and the fascinating Mining Museum.

What to Pack

Your trainee Pokémon—For a workout in Oreburgh City's Gym.

Your prize Pokémon—For a chance to defeat the Gym Leader and win the prestigious Coal Badge.

Your flashlight—To explore the underground mine caverns. Look out for Pokémon fossils!

SPOT THAT POKÉMON

If you visit the Mining Museum, watch out for prehistoric Pokémon that have been brought back to life. Most are harmless, but some can be ferocious!

Who's Who?

Roark
The Gym Leader of Oreburg Gym and the foreman of the Oreburgh Mine is named Roark. He also loves fossils.

Dr. Kenzo
Dr. Kenzo is the director of the Oreburgh Mining Museum. He oversees the Fossil Restorer Machine.

Armaldo

Rampardos

Bastiodon

Roark

Dr. Kenzo

DID YOU KNOW?

It takes 24 hours to bring a Fossil Pokémon back to life.

TOP 3 MUST SEES

1. Oreburgh Mine
Oreburg Mine is one of the city's key features and its main source of energy. Most of the people who live in Oreburgh City work in the mine.

2. Mining Museum
The Mining Museum tells the story of mining in the area. Its research tower houses many Pokémon fossils.

3. Oreburgh Gym
Oreburg Gym is a training center where Pokémon can work out and practice their battle skills.

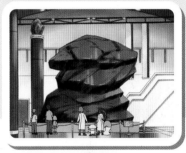

DOS & DON'TS
WITH . . . AERODACTYL

Do use Piplup and Buneary to pin it to the ground.

Don't get in the way of its sharp fangs.

Do ask Dr. Kenzo to help capture it.

Don't let it escape by flying away.

REVIEW:
THE MINING MUSEUM

Had an amazing time at the Mining Museum in Oreburgh City! The fossil and coal exhibits are the best I've ever seen. The Mining Museum's Fossil Research Lab houses an amazing Fossil Restorer Machine. I loved seeing the prehistoric Pokémon Aerodactyl come back to life—even if it did go on a rampage!

FLOAROMA TOWN AND THE VALLEY

Floaroma Town is a beautiful settlement where flowers and plants grow in abundance. Every home seems to have sweet-smelling gardens and brightly colored flower beds. Legend says that long ago, the town was blessed with a radiant floral shower. The nearby windy valley houses a large wind-generated power plant.

Who's Who?

Theresa, Raichu, and Abigail

Abigail and Theresa
Kind Abigail runs her popular bakery with her niece, Theresa. Abigail's talented Raichu, nicknamed Sugar, helps her with the baking!

Forsythia
Forsythia is the owner of Pick a Peck of Colors. She also teaches Trainers to cook Poffins, using berries from her orchard.

Forsythia

SPOT THAT POKÉMON

Many species of Pokémon can be spotted in and around Floaroma. Drifting, creepy Gastly might give you a surprise, and legendary Suicune often appear in bright light. Beware the powerful Thunder Shock move of local Magnemite.

Gastly

Magnemite

Suicune

TOP 3 MUST SEES

1. Pick a Peck of Colors

Floarama Town's florist shop sells flowers of all kinds. The owner also offers cookery classes.

2. Valley Pokémon Center

Don't be put off by the playful Gastly that haunt the entrance—this Pokémon Center is a cozy stopover along the route out of Floarama.

3. Valley Windworks

This wind farm makes power for the area using eight tall wind turbines. Security guard Benjamin protects the farm with a fleet of patrolling Magnemite.

HOW TO MAKE POFFINS

1 Cook the berries in a pan over a high heat.

2 Stir frequently, until the mixture becomes thick and doughy.

3 Pour into poffin molds and allow to cool.

4 Tuck in! Your Pokémon will enjoy them!

TOP FESTIVALS

Floaroma's Pokémon Contest
This contest is held in the flower-filled Contest Hall. Here Coordinators and Pokémon compete for the highly treasured Floaroma Ribbon.

ETERNA CITY

Eterna City is one of the oldest cities in the Sinnoh region. It has many interesting buildings, including the Historical Museum, where you can discover some awe-inspiring exhibits and artifacts. Outside the city is the Eterna Forest, a place of mist, mystery, and enchantment.

DON'T MISS:
ETERNA HISTORICAL MUSEUM

- The Museum's prized artifacts are the powerful **Adamant Orb** and the mysterious **Lustrous Orb**.

- Other exhibits include **impressive statues** of Dialga and Palkia, Legendary Pokémon who are said to have combined to create the Sinnoh region. There are also statues of the Lake Guardians Mesprit, Uxie, and Azelf.

- Visit the model of the **Space-Time Tower**, which is not only a building but also the largest musical instrument in the Pokémon world.

SPOT THAT POKÉMON

Look out for some interesting Bug- and Grass-type Pokémon in Eterna Forest. In Eterna Gym, you'll see Gardenia's agile Turtwig, super-fast Cherubi, and Roserade, with its sweet but toxic aroma.

Roserade

Turtwig

Cherubi

CITY TOURS

Spend the day seeing the top sights in Eterna City or take a day trip to a nearby attraction.

1. Eterna Gym
Eterna Gym specializes in Grass-type Pokémon. Its Gym Leader is Gardenia, who loves catching new Pokémon in the Eterna Forest.

2. Buizel River
This river near Eterna City is home to wild Buizel. Fishing in the river often lures the Pokémon out. But watch out—they might try to drag your fishing rod away!

3. Great Hall
A Pokémon Dress-up Contest takes place yearly in this hall just outside Eterna City. Pokémon imitate other Pokémon by dressing up or doing impressions. The winning Trainer receives a Pokémon Egg.

DID YOU KNOW?

The reward for defeating Gardenia in the Gym is the Forest Badge.

BUIZEL'S TOP MOVES

Water Gun

Aqua Jet

Sonic Boom

PASTORIA CITY

DON'T MISS:
THE GREAT MARSH

- The Great Marsh is a **boggy wetland** where tall grasses sprout from the mud and water.

- Many **unusual and wild Pokémon** hide among the grasses.

- The marsh is the location of the **Pastoria Croagunk Festival**, where Croagunk battle it out to be named champion. Try to see the Croagunk-themed fireworks!

TRAINER TIPS

- The Gym Leader for Pastoria City Gym is named Crasher Wake. He specializes in strong Water-type Pokémon.

- Think about using a Croagunk—they are seen as special guardians of the wetlands and every household in Pastoria City raises one.

- The Pastoria City Gym has a pool with floating platforms on it. The winner of the Gym battle is awarded the Fen Badge.

DID YOU KNOW?

You can walk across the Great Marsh along wooden boardwalks or jump on the passenger train at one of its platforms.

Crasher Wake and his Pokémon

SPOT THAT POKÉMON

The Great Marsh contains Pokémon that are not found anywhere else in the region. Also keep your eyes open for Croagunk—hundreds of these wild Pokémon live here.

Carnivine

Croagunk

Exeggcute

Yanma

NEED TO KNOW:
CELESTIC TOWN

- A Pokémon Contest is held in Celestic Town's Contest Hall—here you might win the prized **Celestic Ribbon**.

- Celestic Town is the hometown of local celebrity, **Sinnoh League Champion Cynthia**.

Celestic Ribbon

SINNOH REGION EXPLORATIONS

Get ready to explore these exciting locations! Pastoria City lies on the edge of a large swamp known as the Great Marsh, which is home to the city's mascot, the wild Croagunk. The City's Gym has an indoor pool with floating islands. Nearby is Celestic Town, a place with a long, rich history in the region.

CELESTIC TOWN

TOP 3 MUST SEES

1. Lila's Fashion Shop
Lila is Celestic Town's world-famous Pokémon Stylist. She designs clothes and accessories for Pokémon and Pokémon Trainers.

2. Celestic Town Historical Research Center
The Research Center studies historical artifacts from the Celestic Ruins next door. One of its most prized discoveries is the mysterious Lustrous Orb.

3. Celestic Town Contest Hall
This beautiful Contest Hall is home to a fierce Pokémon contest. Dawn's mom, Johanna, lost to Lila here, ending a long winning streak.

NORTHERN SINNOH REGION

At the northernmost tip of the Sinnoh region lies Snowpoint City. This picturesque city glistens with snow that blows down from Mount Coronet. Nearby is the busy port settlement of Chocovine Town, which is often crowded with tourists during the annual migration of Phione.

SNOWPOINT CITY

Zoey

Who's Who?

Zoey
A Pokémon Coordinator from Snowpoint City, Zoey likes to win. But she tries not to take it to heart after a loss.

What to Pack

Winter clothing—To keep you warm in chilly Snowpoint City.

A quick brain—For learning at Snowpoint Trainers School.

A fast swimming Pokémon—To compete in the Iceberg Race.

TOP FESTIVALS

Pokémon Iceberg Race
This icy race is an annual event where you race your Pokémon around an iceberg.

CHOCOVINE TOWN

TOP 3 MUST SEES

1. Poké Mart
This store sells a variety of useful items for Pokémon Trainers and Coordinators, like Seals to attach to Poké Balls.

2. Chocovine Water Park
The outdoor water park in Chocovine is a popular tourist attraction, with tropical palm trees around the sides.

3. Chocovine Contest Hall
The grand Chocovine Contest Hall is the place to battle for the chance of winning the Chocovine Ribbon.

SPOT THAT POKÉMON

Alongside the famous Phione, keep an eye out for other Water-type Pokémon in the sea by Chocovine Town.

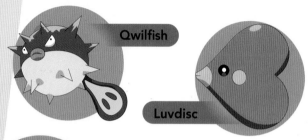

Qwilfish

Luvdisc

Finneon

Phione

DOS & DON'TS
WITH . . . PHIONE

Do ride on a submarine for a chance to see the Phione up close.

Do believe that the Phione are real and not just a myth!

Don't spend all your money on Phione merch (everything from dolls to T-shirts!)

Don't try to capture a Phione in a net—they don't like it.

VEILSTONE CITY AND LAKE VALOR

Veilstone City is a large metropolis in the eastern Sinnoh region. Although it is quite isolated it has many sights, including some half-buried ancient meteorites and a big shopping district. Nearby Lake Valor is a popular tourist attraction, where two tournaments take place in its Contest Hall: The Wallace Cup and the Sinnoh Grand Festival.

Who's Who?

Paul
Paul comes from Veilstone City. He is a super-competitive Pokémon Trainer.

Reggie
Paul's brother Reggie also comes from Veilstone City and is a Pokémon breeder.

Paul

TOP 3 MUST SEES

1. Veilstone Gym
For a chance to win the Cobble Badge, take your Fighting-type Pokémon to Veilstone Gym. Look out for Gym Leader Maylene.

2. Lakeside Resort
Enjoy a touch of luxury with a stay at the Lakeside Resort, overlooking Lake Valor. The top floor of this hotel complex hosts the Welcoming Party for the Grand Festival, where new Top Coordinators are chosen.

3. Seven Stars Restaurant
Make a reservation at this popular eatery for the chance to win a free seven-course meal—if you defeat the owners in a Tag Battle!

SPOT THAT POKÉMON

See Pokémon at Lake Valor, including flocks of Staravia and swarms of melodic Kricketune. Watch out for Paul and his Electabuzz!

Staravia

Electabuzz

Kricketune

DON'T MISS:
THE WALLACE CUP

- This special **worldwide competition** is held once a year in different locations.

- Pokémon Coordinators compete for the prestigious **Aqua Ribbon**—which grants immediate access to any other Grand Festival worldwide.

- It is named after Wallace, a famous Contest Master who acts as the **host and judge** of each competition.

The Wallace Cup judges

TRAINER TIPS

Lake Valor

- Take a break from competitions and visit the sparkling Lake Valor.

- The lake is home to Azelf—a powerful Psychic-type Pokémon and Lake Guardian.

- There is a secret entrance under Lake Valor which leads to the Lake Guardian's home.

HEARTHOME CITY AND MOUNT CORONET

Hearthome City is a busy metropolis and the fifth largest city in the entire Pokémon world. On the way to Hearthome City, you can't miss snow-topped Mount Coronet, the tallest peak in the Sinnoh region's mountain range.

REVIEW: THE HEARTHOME COLLECTION FASHION SHOW

☺☺☺☺☺

The Hearthome Collection is my favorite fashion show! I saw my hero, Lady Cocoa—her fashion is totally amazing. This year they handed out an award for the most unique outfit, an accessory award, and a grand winner. It's so fun seeing all the outfits, grooming, and moves Trainers and their Pokémon show off.

TOP 3 MUST SEES

1. Amity Square
In this park north of Hearthome City, spend a few moments wandering the old ruins dedicated to the Legendary Pokémon Dialga and Palkia.

2. Hearthome Stadium
The huge Hearthome Stadium hosts Hearthome City's biggest attractions. The Tag Battle Competition is always attended by Mayor Enta.

3. Hearthome Gym
This Gym is based on Ghost-type Pokémon. If you can defeat fabulous Gym Leader Fantina, the Relic Badge will be yours!

SPOT THAT POKÉMON

Lots of cute and interesting Pokémon are found in bustling Hearthome City, including furry Eevee, fluffy Buneary, Fairy-type Clefairy, and Water-type Psyduck. But Mount Coronet is the only place in the region where you can find wild herds of armored Shieldon.

Buneary

Clefairy

Eevee

Psyduck

DID YOU KNOW?

Hearthome Stadium hosts the hugely popular Tag Battle Competition. The prize is two Soothe Bells, whose beautiful sound inspires peace and joy.

Shieldon

DOS & DON'TS
WITH . . . SHIELDON

Do look for these wild Pokémon in the forests around Mount Coronet.

Don't even think about battling Shieldon. It can use its tough armored head to defend itself.

Do feed them their favorite foods, which are grass, berries, and tree roots.

Don't let ruthless Hunter J capture them and sell them on the black market.

LEGENDARY AND MYTHICAL

The Sinnoh region has magical lakes, fiery volcanoes, and unpredictable other-dimensional worlds. They are all home to incredible Legendary and Mythical Pokémon. Prepare to meet some of the most unusual Pokémon in the Pokémon world!

Darkrai
Type: Dark
Height: 4 ft 11 in (1.5 m)
Darkrai can cause people and Pokémon to fall asleep and have terrifying nightmares.

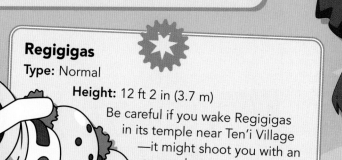

Regigigas
Type: Normal
Height: 12 ft 2 in (3.7 m)
Be careful if you wake Regigigas in its temple near Ten'i Village —it might shoot you with an energy beam.

Arceus
Type: Normal
Height: 10 ft 6 in (3.2 m)
Known as "The Original One," Arceus is said to have created the Sinnoh region and possibly the whole Pokémon world.

Palkia

Type: Water-Dragon
Height: 13 ft 9 in (4.2 m)
Said to live in a parallel dimension, Palkia has the ability to distort space.

Dialga

Type: Steel-Dragon
Height: 17 ft 9 in (5.4 m)

It is an ancient legend in the Sinnoh region that Dialga has the power to control time.

Cresselia

Type: Psychic
Height: 4 ft 11 in (1.5 m)

This Legendary Pokémon has the power to chase away nightmares caused by Dark-type Mythical Darkrai. It can be spotted on a small island off the north coast of the Sinnoh region called Fullmoon Island.

HIDDEN CORNERS

The Sinnoh region's hidden corners are worth exploring. As well as its exciting cities and beautiful countryside, the region has many smaller towns and villages, where life is more relaxed. Off the coast, a group of small islands are connected by bridges. They can be reached by airship.

REGION TOP EXPERIENCES

TOP TASTE EXPERIENCE

Try Miltank milk. Drop into the Mountain Hut Maid Café on the road to Veilstone City to sample this delicious drink.

Mountain Hut Maid Café

TOP CULTURAL EXPERIENCE

Travel by blimp to Canalave City, on an island off the coast of the Sinnoh region. This port city has a chateau, a library, and many canals and bridges.

Canalave Library

Old Chateau

TOP WILD POKÉMON EXPERIENCE

Seek wild Pokémon on remote Iron Island, accessible only by ship from Canalave City.

Port and town

Iron Island

SPOT THAT POKÉMON

The Summit Ruins near Mount Coronet are haunted by many types of Ghost-type Pokémon, including Gastly, Haunter, Gengar, Shuppet, and Misdreavous.

Shuppet

Misdreavous

Gengar

Flint, Bertha, Aaron, and Lucian

Who's Who?

The Elite Four
At one of the Sinnoh region's top tournaments, the Champion League, competitors have to face the "Elite Four" —the top four Trainers in the region.

DOS & DON'TS
WITH . . . UNOWN

Do seek Unown at Solaceon Ruins. Each Unown is shaped like a letter in an ancient alphabet.

Don't forget that Unown can read your thoughts and feelings.

Do be careful of their ability to distort reality.

Don't frighten them. Unown are very timid.

Unown

UNOVA REGION

The Unova region's big, busy cities are surrounded by calm, beautiful forests. From sunny seaside spots and ancient Pokémon ruins to modern movie theaters, this region has something for everyone!

NUVEMA TOWN

A small town nestled between a forest and a harbor, Nuvema Town is a Pokémon Trainer's first port of call in the region. It is here that they will find Professor Juniper and receive their first Unova Pokémon.

Unova Pokédex

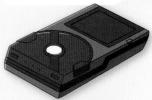

What to Pack

Xtranceiver—To ask Professor Juniper any questions you might have, even when you've moved on to the next town.

Pikachu—Considered rare in the Unova region, Pikachu is sure to make a big impression wherever you go!

Pokédex—The Unova region Pokédex is slim and small enough to fit in your pocket!

Who's Who?

Professor Juniper
Young, friendly, and an expert on Pokémon origins, Professor Juniper welcomes Ash to the Unova region and becomes a firm friend.

Bianca
Bianca is an enthusiastic but scatter-brained Pokémon Trainer. She has her clumsy moments, but she still manages to collect all eight badges!

Trip
Trip is a Pokémon Trainer who cares about only one thing: winning.

Professor Cedric Juniper
Professor Juniper's dad is also a professor, though he prefers to conduct his research outside of the lab.

Professor Juniper

Bianca

Trip

TOP 3 MUST SEES

1. Professor Juniper's Lab
Home to some of the professor's fascinating research into where Pokémon come from.

2. Harbor
A large harbor dominates the city's coastline. It is always bustling with tourists, Trainers, and shoppers.

3. Airport
Nuvema has its own airport. You can't miss the tall air traffic control tower, rising high over the runway.

FIRST PARTNER POKÉMON

Trainers looking for their Unova region first partner Pokémon will be excited to choose from Snivy, Tepig, and Oshawott.

Snivy

Oshawott

Tepig

DOS & DON'TS
WITH . . . OSHAWOTT

Do encourage Oshawott to keep training.

Don't worry if its scalchop seashell gets damaged in battle—Oshawott can regrow it!

Do ask Oshawott to help you crack open berries with its scalchop seashell.

Don't get a surprise when it bursts out of its own Poké Ball to battle!

OPELUCID CITY AND VILLAGE OF DRAGONS

Opelucid City is a large, modern city and the place to be if you want to become a Dragon Master, thanks to the prestigious Opelucid Academy. Nearby is the small Village of Dragons, where Dragon-type Pokémon are honored.

Zweilous

Axew

SPOT THAT POKÉMON

The Elder of the Village of Dragons gives young residents Dragon-type Pokémon to raise. That's how Iris got her Axew, and where Shannon got the two Zweilous she is raising.

Who's Who?

Iris
This tough Pokémon Trainer dreams of adventure, travel, and becoming a Dragon Master.

Shannon
Shannon is a childhood friend of Iris and a Pokémon breeder. Like Iris, she dreams of traveling the world.

Drayden
Opelucid Gym Leader and principal of the Opelucid Academy, Drayden is a dragon expert and fierce battle opponent.

Iris

Shannon

Drayden

TRAINER TIPS

- Head to Opelucid Gym to battle for the Legend Badge.

- The battlefield is in a dark, candlelit room with statues of Dragon-type Pokémon on the walls.

- Gym Leader Drayden is very observant. He will often wait to see what moves his opponents make before blocking them and using a powerful counter-attack.

Opelucid Gym arena

TOP 3 MUST SEES

1. Opelucid Academy
One of the best training schools in the Unova region. Don't miss a tour of its beautiful grounds.

2. Opelucid Gym
Opelucid Gym is a dramatic-looking, tall stone pyramid flanked by two stone dragon statues.

3. Legendary Dragon Statues
Statues of Reshiram and Zekrom stand in the center of the Village of Dragons—a symbol of how much the residents admire the Dragon-type Pokémon.

NEED TO KNOW:
IRIS

- Iris is rarely seen without her **Axew**. You can usually find it riding in her hair!

- Iris finds **Gym Leader Drayden** intimidating, but he thinks she's good enough to be the next Gym Leader.

- Iris is **Champion of the Unova League**.

UNIQUE POKÉMON ENVIRONMENTS

The Unova region is home to lots of big, busy cities and popular tourist attractions. But there are many calm, quiet spots that are not as well known. It is in places like these that visitors can observe their favorite Pokémon, learn fascinating new things, and witness unique wonders.

SAWSBUCK FOREST

Somehere near Driftveil City is a mysterious, fog-shrouded forest where Deerling and Sawsbuck roam. Rumor has it that it's possible to see all four seasonal forms of Sawsbuck at once, if you find just the right spot.

DID YOU KNOW?

Deerling and its Evolution, Sawsbuck, change forms depending on the season. Deerling's fur changes color and scent, while Sawsbuck's horns blossom with seasonal plants.

FLOCCESY RANCH

A flock of tame Mareep live at the quiet, family-run Floccesy Ranch, which is near the White Ruins. They are guarded by an Ampharos, who has only recently found the confidence to control the flock.

Mareep

FERROSEED RESEARCH INSTITUTE

Not far from Opelucid City is the renowned Ferroseed Research Institute. The institute studies the moss produced by Ferroseed, which is said to enhance a Pokémon's abilities.

DID YOU KNOW?

Professor Malveaux, leader of the Ferroseed Research Institute, once returned to the institute to discover the whole building covered in moss!

RAINBOW VALLEY

Cottonee

Tourists who want to witness something unforgettable must make sure to visit Rainbow Valley after a full moon. After finding their partner, Cottonee float through the valley on the Diamond Breeze. The surrounding mountains glisten in rainbow colors.

STRIATON CITY

The big city of Striaton has tall skyscrapers, a large Pokémon Center, and lots of shops, including a bustling market. Trainers visit the city to battle at the grand Striaton Gym and to enjoy a meal at the city's top restaurant.

Connoisseurs of Unova
Pokémon Connoisseurs assess the relationship between a Trainer and their Pokémon to see how well they work together and what can be improved.

DID YOU KNOW?

Cilan and his brothers love food so much that they have included a fancy restaurant at Striaton Gym.

?

Who's Who?

Professor Fennel
A brilliant professor, Fennel studies dreams and the hidden powers within them.

Cilan
One of the three Striaton Gym Leaders, Cilan is very impressed by Ash's battle style. He even asks to join Ash on his travels.

Professor Fennel

Cilan

DON'T MISS:
THE DREAMYARD

- The Dreamyard is an old Pokémon **energy research facility** just outside the city.

- The site used to be a Pokémon Energy Laboratory before it **exploded**.

- The site researched Musharna, the Drowsing Pokémon, which **eats people's dreams** and emits a **Dream Mist** from its forehead.

- **Professor Fennel** used to work at the Pokémon Energy Laboratory, trying to turn Musharna's Dream Mist into a **pure energy source**.

NEED TO KNOW: CILAN

- He is a **triplet**. His two brothers are named Chili and Cress, and all three of them are Gym Leaders.

- He enjoys playing **harmless pranks**.

- If there's one thing Cilan loves as much as Pokémon, it's food! He's an **incredible chef** and describes pretty much everything as if it's a meal.

- As well as being a Trainer and Gym Leader, Cilan is also a **Pokémon Connoisseur**.

TRAINER TIPS

- The Striaton Gym battlefield is concealed behind one wall of the restaurant.

- Trainers need only battle one of the three Gym Leaders, although they can choose to battle all three!

- Defeating two out of the three Gym Leaders will earn you the Trio Badge.

Striaton Gym and Restaurant

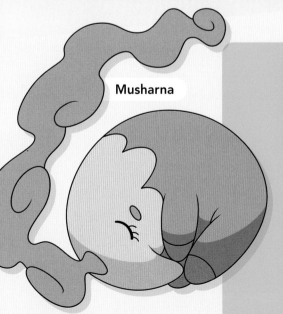

Musharna

DOS & DON'TS
WITH . . . MUSHARNA

Do keep Musharna away from too many negative thoughts, because they can cause it stress.

Don't enter the dark pink mist—it brings people's nightmares to life!

Do look for the Dream Mist emanating from its forehead. The color will tell you what sort of dreams it has eaten.

Don't wake it up if you can help it because Musharna can get grumpy.

DRIFTVEIL CITY

Driftveil City attracts Trainers to its brightly colored Gym. Other tourists visit to wander through the market or enjoy a day at the port, watching the freighters and fishing boats deliver their cargo. Just off the coast is the mythical Island of Legends, Milos Island, which is always worth a visit.

What to Pack

Storage box—For collecting precious and rare Revival Herbs.

Camera—To capture photos of the Shrine of Landorus and the famous obelisks of Thundurus and Tornadus.

Gothorita—To help summon Landorus in case the Legendary Pokémon Thundurus and Tornadus return to wreak havoc on Milos Island!

Gothorita

TOP 3 MUST SEES

1. **Driftveil Drawbridge**
   Driftveil's famous bridge connects the city to Route 5. Many consider the bridge to be the pride of Driftveil.

2. **Driftveil City Market**
   First-time visitors must check out this busy, colorful market where they can meet the locals and taste delicious foods.

3. **Bobby's Day Care**
   Stop by the day care to see Pokémon Eggs and baby Pokémon, and to learn how they are cared for.

NEED TO KNOW:
DRIFTVEIL GYM

- The Gym is located in an **underground mine**.

- Gym Leader Clay has been known to **challenge Trainers** to carry out a task before they can go up against him in battle.

- Clay focuses on **Ground-type Pokémon** and battles are three-on-three matches.

DID YOU KNOW?

A mythical island off the coast of Driftveil City, Milos Island is the only source of Revival Herbs. These have special Pokémon healing powers.

SPOT THAT POKÉMON

There were once rumors of a Klink Evolution in Driftveil, but the only Klink to be found were Klink-shaped cookies! The City is full of Pokémon to spot, from the Durant living in underground tunnels to the Deino staying at Bobby's Day Care. The city is also protected by The Mighty Accelguard, a hero with an Accelgor Pokémon sidekick.

Durant

Klink

Deino

Accelgor

CASTELIA CITY

Visitors love losing themselves in the buzzing activity of Castelia City, the Unova region's business center. Its dazzling skyscraper skyline is impressive, but there is more to explore than the city itself. In the silent sands of the nearby desert lies something completely different: an ancient ruin full of mysterious puzzles.

Top Tip!

Sweet, icy Castelia Cones are a tasty treat which can be bought at a stand in Castelia City.

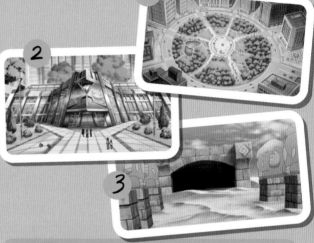

Who's Who?

Kira
This brave Pokémon Ranger knows all about Castelia City and the deserts around it.

Shane Seeker
Shane is a determined Trainer on a mission to collect Shiny or alternate color Pokémon. He travels with his prized Shiny Psyduck.

Kira

Shane Seeker

TOP 3 MUST SEES

1. Central Plaza
This beautiful park at the center of Castelia City has green grass and a famous fountain. It is a place of calm amid the city's bustle.

2. Castelia Gym
Trainers must visit this purple, sloping building and battle Gym Leader Burgh to get the Insect Badge.

3. Colossus Ruins
The ruins of an ancient city can be found in the Desert Resort outside Castelia City. Head here if you think you can solve the puzzles and uncover the Colossus and an ancient chamber of gold!

SPOT THAT POKÉMON

Cofagrigus have been spotted here, and Volcarona have been seen in an abandoned mining town nearby. And if you manage to solve the puzzles of the ruins, you may be lucky enough to meet the Colossus—which is a truly rare giant Golurk!

Volcarona

Cofagrigus

Sandile

DID YOU KNOW?

A group of Venipede once stampeded through Castelia. They emerged from the underground sewer tunnels and ran riot, confused by weird energy.

Golurk

What to Pack

Notepad and paper—To help solve the puzzles of the Colossus Ruins.

Picnic blanket—For a pleasant afternoon snack in Central Plaza.

Surfboards—For an easy (and fun!) way to cross the hot desert sands.

DOS & DON'TS
WITH . . . GIANT GOLURK

Do make the most of its immense strength in battle.

Don't remove Golurk's chest seal, or its energy will run wild!

Do ask Golurk to help you find fossils.

Don't worry if your other Pokémon rest on Golurk—it is very gentle among friends.

NIMBASA CITY

The leisure and entertainment capital of the region, Nimbasa is an exciting metropolis full of fun attractions and interesting tourist spots. It's also home to the Nimbasa Gym and a world-famous subway system run by the Subway Bosses.

Top Tip!

If you come across a spooky-looking mansion, stay away! It's home to a Litwick who can drain life energy from Pokémon and their Trainers.

DID YOU KNOW?

If watching the games at the Big Stadium leaves you wishing you could have a go, head over to the Small Court, where you can play for yourself!

Who's Who?

Subway Bosses
Brothers Ingo and Emmet run the subway through the city. Their trains will take you wherever you want to go!

Elesa
The Nimbasa Gym Leader is also a supermodel. Trainers need to defeat her in battle to win the Bolt Badge.

Don George
Don George is host of the Club Battle, a famous tournament where the winner receives a seven-feather "Top-Class Driftveil Wing Set!"

Subway Bosses

Elesa

Don George

TOP 3 MUST SEES

1. Gear Station
Catch the subway trains and Battle Trains that run across Nimbasa from this gigantic, bustling station.

2. Pokémon Center
The Nimbasa Pokémon Center is the largest in all of the Unova region!

3. Nimbasa Gym
Trainers and tourists alike enjoy visiting the Gym, both to battle for the Bolt Badge and to take in its unusual architecture.

FUN SPORTS

The Stamp Rally
The Subway Bosses' Stamp Rally is a challenge to collect 60 Pokémon stamps in a single day. Whoever achieves this difficult task will get to battle one of the Subway Bosses!

DON'T MISS:
NIMBASA CITY MUSICAL THEATER

- The Musical Theater plays fantastic **musical shows** with Pokémon dancing on stage.

- Remember to stop by the nearby **ferris wheel** for a ride or pop by the **Big Stadium** for a game.

UNDELLA TOWN

Undella Town is a beautiful seaside hotspot and popular holiday resort. It is known for its sparkling seas, golden beaches, and luxurious villas. Nearby, Lacunosa Town is a popular destination for Trainers wishing to compete in the Pokémon World Tournament Junior Cup.

REVIEW:
FLOWER GARDEN TROUPE

This group of performers put on extravagant theater shows with their Pokémon. While they may be elegant, only females are allowed to take part, which isn't very inclusive. And the performers are a little bit snooty as well!

TOP 3 MUST SEES

1. Seaport
Undella Town's seaport is ready to welcome visitors landing from all over the Pokémon world.

2. Cynthia's Villa
Cynthia's villa is a huge, grand building with plenty of guest bedrooms and a balcony with the most perfect view.

3. Undella Bay
The town overlooks Undella Bay, a natural cove where many tourists go in search of golden beaches and the sunken Abyssal Ruins.

NEED TO KNOW: CYNTHIA

- Cynthia is a **famous battle champion** and is an **expert in mythology and legends**.

- She is **truly kind** and will do anything to help her friends and her Pokémon.

- She loves to invite guests to her **beautiful holiday home** in Undella Town.

DID YOU KNOW?

The Pokémon World Tournament Junior Cup is held in nearby Lacunosa Town. The contest sees 16 Trainers battling it out to receive a trophy and the chance to battle against the champion of the Unova Pokémon League.

SPOT THAT POKÉMON

Local Pokémon include Onix, Wingull, and Staryu. Meloetta and Dragonite have also been spotted in Undella Town.

Onix

Staryu

Wingull

DAY TRIP TO ...
UNDELLA BAY

Relax on the beach
Begin the day by relaxing in the sunshine at Undella Bay's beautiful seaside.

Boat tours
Spot huge Wailord off the coast of Undella Bay on a fun boat trip. You can also visit Onix Island a short boat ride away, with stunning beaches, reefs, and a cave where a special Onix lives.

Abyssal Ruins
The best place to visit in the afternoon is the amazing Abyssal Ruins. The Legendary Pokémon Meloetta once sank this ancient city to the seabed—it's a must-see sight on your day out!

NACRENE CITY AND PINWHEEL FOREST

Nacrene City is an artist's paradise. Public art and statues line the streets, the buildings are painted in colorful hues, and stained glass windows throw pretty light at all angles. Outside the city, Pinwheel Forest offers an escape for nature lovers and Pokémon fans.

TOP 3 MUST SEES

1. Nacrene City Museum
This enormous museum houses rare artifacts and unique art. It is a top destination for art lovers.

2. Skyarrow Bridge
The largest bridge in the region connects Pinwheel Forest to Castelia City.

3. Nacrene Battle Club
Trainers and Pokémon can practice and perfect new skills at this well-equipped Battle Club. It has a gymnasium and swimming pool.

Who's Who?

Lenora
This kind, confident Gym Leader lays a series of puzzles for Trainers to complete as they try to find the Gym.

Lenora

Hawes
The vice curator at the museum, Hawes prepares and organizes all the exhibits. If anything goes wrong, he's usually the first to know!

Hawes

DID YOU KNOW?

Before Skyarrow Bridge was built, a young girl named Sally and her Gothitelle used to help her father on his water taxi, ferrying passengers across to Castelia City.

DID YOU KNOW?

The Nacrene City Museum once had an exhibition that appeared to be haunted! It was eventually revealed that a Yamask who had got separated from its mask was behind the strange goings-on.

TRAINER TIPS

- The Nacrene Gym is hidden inside the Nacrene City Museum.

- The entrance to the Gym can be accessed through the museum's library.

- Trainers need to crack a code to figure out how to open up the entrance to the Gym.

NEED TO KNOW:
PINWHEEL FOREST

- Just outside the forest is a **Poké Mart**, where you can get lots of supplies for your next adventure.

- At the center of the forest is a **huge tree**. From the top of it, you can see the whole forest!

- In case your Pokémon need help, there's a **Pokémon Center** inside the forest.

SPOT THAT POKÉMON

Galvantula and Patrat live in the wild in Pinwheel Forest, and Sewaddle have been spotted there too.

Sewaddle

Patrat

Gothitelle

Galvantula

SITES OF POKÉMON MYTHOLOGY

The Unova region has a rich mythology, and contains lots of ruins and ancient sites. The rivalry between Legendary Pokémon Reshiram—the Vast White Pokémon—and Zekrom—the Deep Black Pokémon—is one of the Unova region's most well-known legends.

Top Tip!

Protect the ancient relics, but don't try to use them for personal gain— it will only awaken Pokémon who are much too powerful to control!

WHITE RUINS

Location: Near Dragon Spire Castle, the oldest tower in the Unova region.

Relic: The Light Stone, a treasure containing the fire of Reshiram.

Watch out for: Thieves trying to steal the Light Stone.

NATIVE POKÉMON:

Pidove

Timburr

Conkledurr

Reshiram

HERO'S RUIN

Location: Near Chargestone Cave, a mysterious source of energy.

Relic: The Golden Dark Stone, which can summon Zekrom.

Watch out for: Booby traps and fierce Pokémon Guardians.

NATIVE POKÉMON:

Cofagrigus

Sigilyph

ABYSSAL RUINS

Location: Sunk under Undella Bay.

Relic: The Reveal Glass, which can summon the powerful Pokémon known as the Forces of Nature: Landorus, Thundurus, and Tornadus.

Watch out for: People fighting over the ancient city and the relic.

NATIVE POKÉMON:

Meloetta

DID YOU KNOW?

Milos Island, a small island near Driftveil City, has a shrine to the Forces of Nature, known as the Shrine of Landorus. There you can visit the obelisks of Tornadus and Thundurus.

LEGENDARY AND MYTHICAL

The Unova region is home to many Legendary and Mythical Pokémon—and plenty of mysterious sites here are dedicated to them and their special powers.

Terrakion

Type: Rock-Fighting
Height: 6 ft 3 in (1.9 m)
The Legendary Cavern Pokémon is strong enough to make any rock crumble.

Kyurem

Type: Dragon-Ice
Height: 9 ft 10 in (3 m)
The Legendary Boundary Pokémon has the power of freezing-cold energy.

Reshiram

Type: Dragon-Fire
Height: 10 ft 6 in (3.2 m)
The Legendary Vast White Pokémon burns white hot.

Meloetta

Type: Normal-Psychic
Height: 2 ft (0.6 m)
The Mythical Melody Pokémon has a beautiful voice with a mighty power: it can summon the Forces of Nature.

Thundurus

Type: Electric-Flying

Height: 4 ft 11 in (1.5 m)

The Legendary Bolt Strike Pokémon shoots lightning from its tail.

Landorus

Type: Ground-Flying

Height: 4 ft 11 in (1.5 m)

The Legendary Abundance Pokémon is known as the Guardian of the Fields.

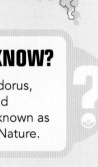

Tornadus

Type: Flying

Height: 4 ft 11 in (1.5 m)

The Legendary Cyclone Pokémon can control the wind.

DID YOU KNOW?

Together, Landorus, Thundurus, and Tornadus are known as the Forces of Nature.

Zekrom

Type: Dragon-Electric

Height: 9 ft 6 in (2.9 m)

The Legendary Deep Black Pokémon can fly through the night unseen, unleashing electricity from its tail.

Genesect

Type: Bug-Steel

Height: 4 ft 11 in (1.5 m)

The Mythical Paleozoic Pokémon was a fossil until it was revived and given a powerful cannon.

UNOVA REGION NEWS

Team Plasma Foiled Again!

International Police arrest members of the mysterious organization known as Team Plasma. Ghetsis, believed to be the group leader, is known for wanting to control all of the Unova region. Researcher Colress and several unnamed grunts were arrested as well. Reports of a Reshiram sighting remain unconfirmed.

UFO Sighting

A number of the Unova region's residents have reported seeing a UFO flying over Area 28. Local alien hunters are looking into this news with interest.

Alder Greets Fans in Nimbasa

Unova Champion Alder surprised fans by chatting and signing autographs for hours. "He's so much nicer than I expected," gushed one young fan. "Yes," agreed another. "Although he kept forgetting my name!"

Clashes Within Team Rocket

Out-of-town gang Team Rocket is rumored to have its sights set on taking over the Unova region, but locals needn't be too worried. Recent reports suggest the team appear to be "blasting off once again."

UNOVA REGION NEWS

VISIT THE POKÉMON WALK OF FAME AT POKÉSTAR STUDIOS!

Walk in the footsteps of all your favorite Pokémon movie stars!

Spotted!

A rare Elgyem was seen around the research lab of Professor Icarus in Area 28. Could this be related to the UFO sightings?

MUSIC REVIEW: KOFFING AND THE TOXICS

As usual, Virbank's local punk rock band do not disappoint. Bassist and frontwoman Roxie and her bandmates played an epic concert last night at Virbank Gym.

Pokéstar Studios Film Competition Winner Announced

Last night, Pokémon Trainer and amateur filmmaker Luke was awarded the Best Picture trophy. Luke's sci-fi blockbuster, *An Epic Defence Force*, wowed the audience. Congratulations to the young winner, who will be given the opportunity to shoot a new movie for Pokéstar Studios!

KALOS REGION

This star-shaped land has three main regions: beautiful Coastal Kalos, the vast Mountain region, and busy Central Kalos. Its capital, Lumiose City, is home to the world-famous Prism Tower. The region is also home to the power of Mega Evolution.

LUMIOSE CITY

Known for its art and architecture, this vibrant city is a center of culture, sport, and tourism. It is also known for its tradition of invention, fashion, and even Pokémon grooming.

Top Tip!

No Pokémon Trainer would want to miss a visit to Professor Sycamore's Lab. He studies the mysteries of Mega Evolution and keeps a special Pokémon habitat!

Who's Who?

Clemont
The Gym Leader of Lumiose, Clemont, is a keen inventor who believes that "the future is now, thanks to science!"

Bonnie
Clemont's younger sister loves cute Pokémon. She feels protective of her brother and is always trying to find him a future wife.

Serena
Ash's friend since childhood days at summer camp, talented Serena is gifted at fashion and destined to become a top Pokémon Performer.

Serena

Clemont

Bonnie

1

2

3

TOP 3 MUST SEES

1. Prism Tower
This tower's shimmering surface lights up the city. It is a symbol of the region across the world.

2. Lumiose Museum
Displaying the great works of art of the Kalos region, this historic museum attracts countless tourists every year. It also attracts the occasional thief, like robot-inventor, Belmondo!

3. Lumiose Conference Stadium
This arena is home to the Lumiose Conference, the big Pokémon competition of the region. It hosts the all-important finals, watched by huge crowds.

DID YOU KNOW?

?

Near Lumiose City is Vaniville Town, Serena's home, which has all the charm of a typical small Kalos town. She also trained to ride Rhyhorn here!

TRAINER TIPS

- The gym is located in Lumiose Tower, in the center of the city.

- It was once controlled by Clembot, a robot invented by Clemont that went wrong and drove away anyone without four gym badges, including Ash.

- It is now run by Clemont and a reprogrammed Clembot—with a sunnier attitude!

Clembot

ANISTAR CITY, MOUNTAINS, AND VALLEYS

There is something for everyone in this area of contrasts. Modern cities with the latest in entertainment trends lie side by side with mountains that hold ancient secrets and clandestine warrior sects.

TASTY FOODS
PURE PLEASURE PUFFS

A delicious sweet treat, Poké Puffs are a specialty of this area. They come in a dizzying variety of multi-colored icing styles, and are loved by people and Pokémon.

Shauna with Bulbasaur

Nini

Aria

Who's Who?

Shauna
Best friend to Serena and also a rival performer, Shauna is a quirky character who loves to entertain crowds and post videos on Pokévision.

Nini
A regular showcase performer, Nini is yet to win at Master Class level. She loves to perform with Farfetch'd and Smoochum.

Aria
This top Pokémon Performer won the title of Kalos Queen. Aria performs with her Pokémon, Braixen. She is an inspiration to Serena and many others.

TOP 3 MUST SEES

1. Anistar Sundial

This beautiful creation is a major tourist attraction. In fact, it is a source of incredible power, connected to the process of Mega Evolution. Team Rocket once tried to steal it— and failed, of course!

2. Pokémon Showcase Theater

A must-visit if you love to be entertained by the top Pokémon Performers. Here you can see them appear in shows with special themes, like a Pokémon quiz.

3. Ninja Village

Located in a caldera—a volcanic crater—this unique dwelling place is home to a secretive ninja community. Those lucky enough to visit will witness great powers and amazing duels.

SPOT THAT POKÉMON

This is an exciting area for discovering unusual Pokémon. Moltres, a Legendary Bird Pokémon, can be found at nearby Mount Molteau. Skarmory can be spotted at the Sky Relay and Greninja can been seen at the Ninja Village.

Skarmory

Moltres

Greninja

DON'T MISS:
THE SKY RELAY

- A major event in the Anistar area, this **relay race** is for flying Pokémon, who must carry a sash though many obstacles, passing it on to their teammates.

- Ash competed in this race with his Pokémon **Noibat**, **Fletchinder**, and **Hawlucha**.

- Team Rocket cheated at this event with a **mechanical Pelipper**! Of course, it soon fell to pieces.

UNIQUE POKÉMON ENVIRONMENTS

The Kalos region boasts some exceptional Pokémon environments, from the out-and-out fantasy of Pikachuland to the chilly heights of the mountains. If you are ready to rumble on a Rhyhorn, Odyssey Village is a must!

FROST CAVERN

Icy places like the Frost Cavern are a challenge for humans, but many Pokémon, like Snover and Abomasnow, the Frost Tree Pokémon, are perfectly adapted to such sites. Also good in wintry conditions are the sturdy Mamoswine, who have thrived there for over 10,000 years.

Abomasnow

Mamoswine

Snover

ODYSSEY VILLAGE

For a thrilling experience, pay a visit to Odyssey Village where they specialize in Rhyhorn racing. Races start at the village and all the gear can be obtained there. Typically, six Rhyhorn, mounted by Trainers, race along a local route cleared of all other traffic.

Rhyhorn is a Ground- and Rock-type Pokémon. When riding, follow the advice of Serena's mother: "Be one with the Rhyhorn." Don't be afraid of them. Their armored bulk hides a kind heart and affectionate nature.

PIKACHULAND

Join Pikachu fans Frank and Jean to make a blockbuster movie set in Pikachuland. Which Pikachu will save the day against the evil Pikachu Libre?

Who's Who?

Frank
This movie director insists he is the biggest Pikachu fan. He wants to share his love of the Pokémon with the world, via movies!

Jean
Frank's granddaughter, Jean, is devoted to helping make his movie dreams come true. She is a skillful camera operator, makeup artist, and editor.

Cosplay Pikas
Frank has five of these talented Pikachu to dress up and play multiple Pika-parts in his Pika-movie!

Frank

Jean

Cosplay Pikas

Super Pikachu

Pikachu

DOS & DON'TS
WITH . . . POKÉMON MOVIE-MAKING

Do have lots of Pokémon working behind the scenes. Heliolisk, Magnemite, and Swirlix are great at lighting effects.

Don't turn down any useful offers of help. Clemont, for example, turns up in Pikachuland with technical savvy and cool ideas for the film.

Do make sure you have an amazing star, like Ash's Pikachu, to play your lead and a cool hero, like Super Pikachu!

Don't forget to add the bloopers at the end. The fans love to see funny mistakes and behind the scenes foul-ups!

COUMARINE CITY

You will feel very close to nature in this beautiful city, set in a calm, sheltered bay. Here, the mild climate is perfect for the growing of enormous trees and the thriving of Grass-type Pokémon.

Top Tip!

The one millionth passenger on the monorail gets a rare blue ribbon as a prize!

NEED TO KNOW:
MONORAIL

- When **discovering this city**, the best way to travel is by monorail.

- The monorail is not only the **quickest** way to explore, but also provides some **breathtaking views**!

- It **connects both sides of the city**, saving you a hike over the hills.

TYPICAL WEATHER

While the area is generally blessed with balmy weather, a visit from Vanillish and Vanilluxe can bring a sudden snowstorm if they are using Blizzard to show rage or fight a foe. This can happen if Vanillite is in danger, perhaps from thieves like Team Rocket!

DID YOU KNOW?

The Pokémon Showcase Theater is where Pokémon Performers compete to win a coveted Princess Key. You need three keys to compete for the title of Kalos Queen!

SPOT THAT POKÉMON

Grass-type Pokémon abound in this area. Jumpluff, the Cotton Weed Pokémon, can be found here, with Weepinbell and Victreebel also a common sight. The Pokémon Sunflora is always a sunny face to watch out for.

Jumpluff

Sunflora

Weepinbell

Victreebel

TRAINER TIPS

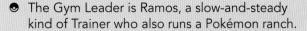

- The Coumarine Gym is well worth a visit. It's in a stunning location—on top of a giant tree!

- The Gym Leader is Ramos, a slow-and-steady kind of Trainer who also runs a Pokémon ranch.

- Expect Ramos to offer you tea or invite you to do some gardening. He wants you to take your time and think in new ways.

TOP FESTIVALS

Coumarine City Festival
The tallest tree in the city was planted years ago by a Trainer and their beloved Pokémon in honor of their great friendship. It is now the center of a festival at which Trainers give gifts to their Pokémon. These don't need to be expensive; they can be homemade or berries picked from the trees.

Coumarine Gym

SHALOUR CITY

This is the place to visit if you want to know more about Mega Evolution, or maybe even Mega Evolve your own Pokémon. For sheer spectacle you must visit the awe-inspiring vastness of nearby Kalos Canyon, where a unique sport takes place.

DID YOU KNOW?

The area near Shalour City offers one out-of-this-world activity you won't find anywhere else—alien spotting! Some believe you can see aliens from Grace Tower, an amazing natural rock formation.

Who's Who?

Korrina
Fond of roller-skating and Fighting-type Pokémon, Korrina is the Shalour City Gym Leader. With her Lucario, she beat Ash in their first battle, but later lost to him at the Shalour Gym.

Moria
A Sky Trainer, based at Kalos Canyon, Moria introduces visiting Trainers to the concept of Sky Battles. Moria's Pokémon is Talonflame, the Scorching Pokémon.

Korrina

Moria

TOP 3 MUST SEES

1. Kalos Canyon
One of the most memorable sites in all of the Kalos region, this epic landscape is a magnet for climbers, artists, and Pokémon Trainers. Formed millennia ago, it has been scoured by wind and weather into majestic rock formations.

2. The Tower of Mastery
A dramatic coastal location means you can only visit the tower and its Gym at low tide. It is said to be the site of the first Mega Evolution.

3. Mega Island
This mysterious isle suddenly appeared one day and is a source of Mega Stones—needed for Pokémon to achieve Mega Evolution. This is a great place to spot Pokémon capable of this exciting transformation.

DID YOU KNOW?

For Flabébé to fly, the little Pokémon must cling on to a Fairy Flower to get airborne. These much-prized flowers are found in the high plains near Shalour and Calanthe Town.

Gurkinn with Mega Alakazam

NEED TO KNOW:
TOWER OF MASTERY

- The Tower is home to the mysterious **Scroll of Secrets**, which is really a set of rules of behavior.

- You could meet the **Mega Evolution Sage** here. It is actually Korrina's grandfather, Gurkinn.

- You can win a coveted **Rumble Badge** at the Tower of Mastery if you defeat Korrina in battle.

FUN SPORTS

Sky Battles
Unique to Kalos Canyon, these thrilling Pokémon battles take place in the air. The winds that flow through the canyon create updrafts perfect for Flying-type Pokémon to ride on. Trainers must wear special wing suits to keep up with the action!

TOP 3 MUST SEES

1. Geosenge Town
This old town is surrounded by unusual rock formations and mountain caves. It is full of people selling the unique Evolution stones.

2. Pomace Mountain
Breathe the fresh mountain air and discover a wonderful world of wildflowers in this peaceful retreat.

3. Geosenge Cave
Rare Mega Stones can be found in the beautiful caves near Geosenge. But watch out for powerful Pokémon inside!

DON'T MISS: FLOWER ARRANGING

- Try a **popular activity** in the area: flower arranging!

- Trainer Mabel will guide you, at her treehouse on **Pomace Mountain**.

- Mabel will show you how flower arrangements **reveal your personality**. Work closely with your Pokémon and discover if you are compatible.

Top Tip!

Other great sites to see on Pomace Mountain are the atmospheric bamboo forest, waterfall, and gentle stream.

NEED TO KNOW: THE CUSSLER SHIPWRECK

- Just off the Muraille coast there is a **sunken cruise ship**, the *Cussler*.

- The intriguing sight was once a luxury liner until it **hit an iceberg** and sank.

- The wreck is said to hold **treasure**, and is home to a variety of curious **sea life**.

MURAILLE COAST AND MOUNTAINS

Nature's wonders will dazzle you in this delightful coastal region, abundant with Water Pokémon and attractions, like its famous shipwreck. Just inland, beautiful snow-topped mountains rise above flower-filled valleys.

SPOT THAT POKÉMON

The sea here contains Qwilfish, the Balloon Pokémon, and ink-spraying Octillery. Mock Kelp Pokémon also abound, like Skrelp and its evolved form, Dragalge.

Quilfish

Octillery

Skrelp

Dragalge

What to Pack

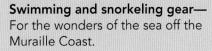

Swimming and snorkeling gear— For the wonders of the sea off the Muraille Coast.

Your pocket money—Evolution stones are for sale in the many shops of Geosenge Town.

Plenty of antidote to Toxic Attack— In case Skrelp takes a dislike to you swimming nearby. Or at least the address of the local Pokémon Center, where they will cure you.

DID YOU KNOW?

The best way to see the wonders of the deep is by submarine. Team Rocket have their own Magikarp-styled version. Unlike them, try to avoid battles with undersea Pokémon and getting caught in whirlpools!

AMBRETTE TOWN

A pretty seaside spot, Ambrette Town is also the location of many extraordinary fossils. Home to a fascinating aquarium too, it is now an area of major interest in the field of natural history.

REVIEW:
AMBRETTE AQUARIUM

I love going to the Ambrette Aquarium! It has the best Magikarp exhibit I have ever seen, and watching all the Water-type Pokémon is so relaxing. I never knew there were so many different types!

Who's Who?

Alexa
This journalist from Lumiose City pops up in the Ambrette area, which she finds fascinating. She loves to travel and has met Ash many times, in many places!

Rodman
An expert angler, Rodman is the curator of the Ambrette Aquarium. He is dedicated to sharing his love of the sea with others and catches Pokémon to display.

Alexa

Rodman

SPOT THAT POKÉMON

Thanks to the Ambrette Fossil Laboratory, many prehistoric Pokémon can be seen in the area. Amaura and Aurorus have been recreated from frozen remains in the lab's freezer room. Tyrunt can sometimes be found roaming in the wild.

Amaura

Aurorus

Tyrunt

DID YOU KNOW?

Many come to seek the giant Golden Magikarp, which according to local legend helps those in trouble at sea. It has often been glimpsed, but never caught!

TRAINER TIPS

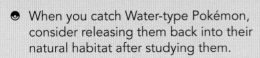

- When you catch Water-type Pokémon, consider releasing them back into their natural habitat after studying them.

- Warning—not all seaside life likes attention. Don't annoy Clauncher, who can blast you with Water Gun and Bubble Beam.

- Don't mistake Team Rocket's fish-shaped submarine for the mythical Golden Magikarp!

Golden Magikarp-shaped submarine

LAVERRE CITY

If you like unforgettable experiences, this is the area for you—with the chance of seeing ghosts, a robot, and the secrets of making Poké Balls. All this and high fashion, too!

TOP EVENTS

Laverre City Fashion Show
There is a vibrant fashion scene in Laverre City, with local Gym Leader Valerie launching her own designs in stunning shows. Her specialty is fashions based on Pokémon like Gothorita and Chimecho. Go along and you may even be asked to model!

DON'T MISS:
THE POKÉ BALL FACTORY

- Travel a short distance from Laverre City to the **Poké Ball Factory**.

- You can visit the **main production room**, and Pokémon can try out the Luxury Ball!

- Beware of being offered a fake **Premium Brand** tour by Team Rocket —who will only be there to try and steal something!

Top Tip!

At Laverre Gym, you might be asked to take part in a Double Battle. The key to winning is the close teamwork between your own Pokémon, so always train together!

SPOT THAT POKÉMON

At the famous Scary House in this area you may well be haunted by Gastly, a Ghost- and Poison-type Pokémon. Others ready to give you the creeps are Haunter and Gengar!

Gastly

Gengar

Haunter

DAY TRIP TO ...
THE CHAPMAN RESEARCH LABORATORY

Robon the robot

Derelict lab
Spend the day exploring a real scientist's lab at environmental scientist Chapman's Research Lab. The lab has fallen into disrepair since Chapman came down with an illness. The work has since been taken over by Chapman's robot Robon and Robon's guard Chesaught.

Afternoon in the desert
Learn how a long-lost spring can restore life to a desert and take part in replanting a forest to make the world a greener place. Robon has been trying to plant trees here for a long time!

HISTORIC CASTLES

The Kalos region is renowned worldwide for the splendor of its castles and palaces. The scene of historic deeds in days gone by, they are still places of adventure and excitement today.

SHABBONEAU CASTLE

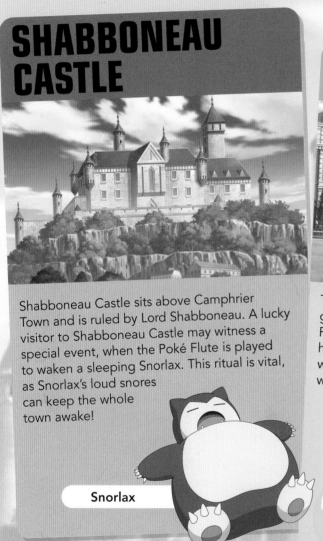

Shabboneau Castle sits above Camphrier Town and is ruled by Lord Shabboneau. A lucky visitor to Shabboneau Castle may witness a special event, when the Poké Flute is played to waken a sleeping Snorlax. This ritual is vital, as Snorlax's loud snores can keep the whole town awake!

Snorlax

PARFUM PALACE

The Parfum Palace is the grand home of the spoiled Princess Allie. The palace has its own battlefield, where the Princess battles with her Furfrou.

Furfrou

DID YOU KNOW?

Princess Allie likes to think everything in the Kalos region belongs to her. She also enjoys making deals that she doesn't plan to keep!

Princess Allie

GLOIRE CITY CASTLE

Gloire City Castle hosts Pokémon Showcases at Masterclass level. Here you might see Delphox, a Fire- and Psychic-type Pokémon, Vivillon the Scale Pokémon, and Aromatisse the Fragrance Pokémon.

Delphox

Vivillon

Aromatisse

CASTLE OF CHIVALRY

If you want to evolve your Pokémon then take it to the Knight Medal Challenge at the Castle of Chivalry. In the Labyrinth of Doubt it will face tests that will take it to a new level of Chivalry.

? DID YOU KNOW?

Wikstrom, a member of the Kalos Elite Four, helps Pokémon evolve by giving them challenges in the castle.

What to Pack

Your camera or Rotom Phone— You will certainly want to take pictures of these majestic monuments.

A spare leek—If you are taking your Farfetch'd to the Knight Medal Challenge, it might need one.

Earplugs—In case the Snorlax near Shabboneau Castle has gone back to sleep.

Farfetch'd

KALOS REGION DISCOVERIES

Situated among rugged peaks and surrounded by Winding Woods, Snowbelle city is the perfect place for lovers of fresh air and amazing scenery. Alternatively on the region's coastline, you can join Professor Sycamore's Summer Camp and make discoveries at the Reflection Cave.

SNOWBELLE CITY

TRAINER TIPS

- ☻ Snowbelle City Gym is worth visiting for its stunning mountain location.

- ☻ Gym Leader Wulfric specializes in Ice-type Pokémon like Abomasnow and Avalugg.

- ☻ The battlefield is made of ice—so be careful you don't slip up!

SPOT THAT POKÉMON

The Winding Woods offer a chance to see many Pokémon, including Spewpa, who lives among the shadows of the thickets. There is also Budew, the Bud Pokémon, and Zigzagoon, the Tiny Raccoon Pokémon. Sentret can be found, too, standing guard.

Budew

Zigzagoon

Spewpa

Sentret

COASTAL KALOS

DON'T MISS:
SUMMER CAMP

- The perfect holiday option in **Coastal Kalos** is to join Professor Sycamore's fun Summer Camp!

- At the camp you are put into teams and share challenges like **orienteering**, **fishing**, **video making**, and **battle practice**. They all help Trainers to bond with their Pokémon.

- Students are given a **cabin** for the duration of the Summer Camp.

Professor Sycamore

Ash visiting the Mirror World

Top Tip!

The mysterious Reflection Cave is not too far from the seaside location where Professor Sycamore holds the annual Pokémon Summer Camp.

DOS & DON'TS
OF . . . THE MIRROR WORLD

Do take care if you go to visit Reflection Cave. It can lead you into another world!

Don't be surprised if you see your mirror-self there—an opposite version of you.

Do expect a surprise if you meet any friends—the mirror versions might not be so friendly!

Don't stay too long. Get out by sunset or you will be trapped there!

LEGENDARY AND MYTHICAL

With its illustrious history, the Kalos region has many Legendary and Mythical Pokémon. It is always exciting to see these powerful and fascinating creatures.

Yveltal

Type: Dark-Flying

Height: 19 ft (5.8 m)

When it spreads out its wings and tail feathers, this Destruction Pokémon can absorb the life force of other living things.

Xerneas

Type: Fairy

Height: 9 ft 10 in (3 m)

The Legendary Life Pokémon has been glimpsed through the fog at the Pokémon Summer Camp. It is said to be able to grant immortality.

DID YOU KNOW?

Yveltal can turn Pokémon and people into stone. When Yveltal comes to the end of its life it returns to slumber in its cocoon form, waiting to awaken.

Volcanion

Type: Fire-Water

Height: 5 ft 7 in (1.7 m)

This rare Pokémon uses a blast of steam to remove obstacles in its path. Make sure that isn't you!

Diancie

Type: Rock-Fairy

Height: 2 ft 4 in (0.7 m)

This Pokémon can create jewels from thin air. Its transformation into jewel form is said to be the most beautiful sight in the world.

Hoopa

Type: Psychic-Ghost

Height: 1 ft 8 in (0.5 m)

This mischievous Mythical Pokémon loves stealing shiny things, especially gold and silver. Although greedy, it does have a kind side.

Zygarde

Type: Dragon-Ground

Height: 16 ft 5 in (5 m)

This Order Pokémon can monitor and repair damaged ecosystems. Team Flare tried to use its power to lay siege to Lumiose City but failed, fortunately!

COOL KALOS

Sport, fashion, spectacle, fine foods: the Kalos region has a lot to offer! If you fancy a visit, be sure not to miss any of its major attractions. Take a look at this handy guide …

IT'S SHOWTIME …

Build a trip around seeing a Pokémon Showcase. Watch a Master Class with Kalos Queen Aria and Ash's pal Serena. Multiple talents combine in dazzling displays of skill, light, and music—pure Pokémon enchantment!

PAMPER POWER

To treat your Pokémon pal take it to the salon of Sherman, the superstar groomer of Lumiose City. His stylish cuts for Furfrou are the talk of the town. With Sherman and his apprentice Jessica's advice, your Pokémon will look and feel good.

FAN FIESTA

Time your trip to see the Kalos League finals at the Lumiose Conference Stadium. 64 Trainers are whittled down to one for the big final. The amazing opening ceremony alone is worth the visit.

MMM ... MACAROONS

Macaroons are a typical tasty treat of the Kalos region, the sweet aroma from these delights wafts from the best boutique bakeries in every town. Learn how to bake them and take the magic home with you. Clemont's Chespin is an especially big fan of the treats!

TOP 3 MUST STAYS

1. Pokémon Centers
   These Centers are happy to put up visiting Trainers and take care of all your Pokémon needs.

2. The Lost Hotel
   This grand hotel might seem like the perfect place to stay on a rainy night, but not everything is at it seems! Is time travel possible at this stopover? And is there any way to stop the mean hotel owner, Mantel?

3. Battle Chateau
   For a real experience, why not try the Battle Chateau? Here you can practice dueling and aim to win the rank of Duke!

ALOLA REGION

Welcome to this sun-soaked region, which is made up of many beautiful islands. You'll find beaches, forests, volcanoes, and ancient temples here, plus an awesome Pokémon School. Incredible Pokémon abound, from the mystical Island Guardians to the amazing Ultra Beasts.

MELEMELE ISLAND

The cultural and business center of the Alola region, this island is a popular destination with tourists. Bountiful with Pokémon, its seas teem with life like Mareanie and Wishiwashi, while Wingull swoop through the blue skies.

Top Tip!

Looking for a typical Alola region treat? Then you must try malasadas. A kind of doughnut, they are served hot and fresh as a popular street food.

Professor Kukui

Professor Samson Oak

Who's Who?

Professor Samson Oak
Head of the school, Professor Samson Oak loves joining in class games. He is usually seen with Komala, his sleepy Pokémon. He loves making Pokémon puns, and hopes people will "Pyroar" with laughter.

Professor Kukui
This dedicated teacher is full of ideas, like Pokémon swapping, Egg-hatching, and field trips to other islands. His other identity is as the top wrestler the Masked Royal.

Hala
As the Kahuna of Melemele Island, Hala organizes the Island Trials, which are necessary to advance to the Alola League. His grandson Hau is a rival to Ash.

TOP 3 MUST SEES

1. The Pokémon School
This amazing facility and welcoming home to students has a sports field for playing Pokébase, a Tauros race track, and even its own theater. Beneath it is the high-tech base of the Ultra Guardians.

2. Clawmark Hill
Pokémon come to Clawmark Hill to duel and practice their skills away from Trainers. Amazing battles can be witnessed by Pokémon like Lycanroc and Magmar —if you keep a respectful distance.

3. Melemele Forest
This ancient and beautiful forest is home to many Pokémon like Bewear, Stufful, and Mimikyu. To some the forest is a restful paradise; to others it is a place of adventure.

Tapu Koko

What to Pack

Sunhat and sun cream—Sunshine is the typical weather of this tropical region.

Swimsuit and goggles—You won't be able to resist that blue sea for long!

A Pokédex—It's an Alolan inspiration to put a Rotom in your Pokédex to create your own talking Rotom Dex, as an ideal guide.

DOS & DON'TS
WITH . . . TAPU KOKO

Do look out for Melemele's Island Guardian, a rare and magical sight. It is also known as the Island Deity.

Don't be surprised if Tapu Koko wants to duel with you. It loves to bring out potential in others.

Do respect all the Pokémon and nature of the island—or this Guardian gets very angry.

Don't be surprised if it pranks you. Tapu Koko loves to steal baseball caps, throw small objects, and sometimes leave gifts.

HAU'OLI CITY

The first port of call for anyone arriving in the Alola region, Hau'oli City on Melemele Island is a top tourist spot, full of seaside attractions and bustling life. There are lively Pokémon everywhere, from colorful Bruxish in the waves to tall Exeggutor blending into the palm trees.

NEED TO KNOW: GETTING AROUND

- There's no need to hurry in Hau'oli. **Trained Pokémon** will take you around, as is the local custom.

- Sharpedo can take you on a **fun sea trip**, as will the more leisurely Lapras.

- To get across town, you can try a **Tauros taxi**!

Sharpedo water ride

TOP 3 MUST SEES

1. The Beach
Want to see Popplio at play? A big Wailmer smiling in the sea? Perhaps just sip a Pinap juice in the shade? Then don't miss a day at the beach, with resorts, restaurants, rides, and even some Pokémon training in the sun.

2. The Street Market
This bustling traditional market will bring you a real taste of the Alola region with its fresh fruit and vegetables. Don't be surprised to see stallholders share their food with hungry Pipipek—here nature's harvest is for all to enjoy.

3. The Shopping Mall
For a more modern shopping experience, the mall is the place to go. It's the best place to find top quality ice-cream made with finest grade vanilla and fresh cream. Fashion, toys, and cakes are also found here.

SPOT THAT FRIEND

Many of Ash's friends from the Pokémon School hang out in Hau'oli City. Watch out for Lana, lover of Water-type Pokémon, Mallow, who helps at her family's restaurant, and the young inventor Sophocles. And don't forget the shy Lillie and competitive Kiawe.

Lana

Lillie

Sophocles

Kiawe

Mallow

DON'T MISS:
AINA'S KITCHEN

- This typical Alolan **family diner** is run by Abe, father of Mallow. She loves to help out.

- It has been featured on **Alola TV**, with a great review.

- Mallow added a new recipe, **berry-topped Poni radish**, after visiting Poni Island.

Top Tip!

When training a Litten, don't be upset if it is shy at first. It may have its own problems, like caring for a Stoutland! Show it love and trust and it might come round. Eventually, Litten evolves into a cool Torracat.

Litten

ULA'ULA ISLAND

Instantly recognizable with the snowy peak of Mount Lanakila rising above it, Ula'ula Island is a place of contrasts. You can sunbathe on a pretty beach and also travel to the top of the mountain for a snowball fight!

DID YOU KNOW?

If Island Deity, Tapu Bulu, drops a Sitrus Berry for your Pokémon, it is gift to restore its strength.

Who's Who?

Acerola
A friend to everyone on Ula'Ula, Acerola referees Island Trials and helped Ash prepare for his own. As a book-lover, Acerola studies the Island myths.

Nanu
This hard-to-please Kahuna likes to avoid work! Nanu's tough style brings out the best in the Trainers who duel him.

Cerah
This sporting celebrity trains on the island. With her Pokémon, Ninetails, Cerah is famous for her Shooting Star move and is a top sled jumper.

Acerola

Nanu

Cerah

DON'T MISS:
SNOW SPECTACULAR

- Ula'ula is famous for its **Sled Jump** event, an annual contest held on Mount Lanakila.

- Contestants slide down the jump on a **Pokésled**, a Pokémon themed sled.

- The competitors are judged on **length of jump** and **special moves**.

- In a recent contest, **Kahuna Hala** and **Crabominable** won with their fan-floating technique and Kahuna Belly-Drum!

TRAINER TIPS

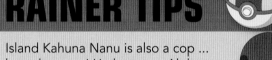

- Island Kahuna Nanu is also a cop ... but a lazy one! He lets stray Alolan Meowth overrun his police station!

- Giovanni, boss of Team Rocket, is one of Nanu's oldest friends. Sometimes he asks the Island Kahuna to grant him a favor.

- When hosting the Island Trials, Nanu only approves of Trainers who can really get their Pokémon to listen to them.

Overrun police station

SPOT THAT POKÉMON

This island is home to Krookodile, the Intimidation Pokémon. You might also spot Mimikins, a ghostly version of Mimikyu, or Crabominable, at home in the mountain snow.

Krookodile

Crabominable

Mimikyu

UNIQUE POKÉMON ENVIRONMENTS

With its many islands and extreme contrasts, the Alola region offers many special environments for its Pokémon, from forest dens to snowy wastes, and sunny valleys to barren peaks.

MOUNT HOKULANI

Look to the sky for special Pokémon on this mysterious mountain on Ula'ula Island.

SPACE TOURS

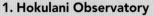

Join this unique night tour to see all the galactic highlights.

1. Hokulani Observatory
From the observatory, you can stargaze at brilliant star formations like the Ninetails and Poipole constellations.

2. Starfall Hill
Starfall Hill is located near the top of Mount Hokulani. The Meteor Pokémon Minior land in abundance on the hill, crack open their shells, and return to the sky in a multi-colored display.

3. Rayquayza and Minior
The Sky High Pokémon can also be seen here, keeping a watch over Minior's return to the stars.

TREASURE ISLAND

Secluded Treasure Island is a haven for wild Pokémon. Watch out for Crabrawler, Cutiefly, and Ribombee.

Crabrawler

Cutiefly

Ribombee

DID YOU KNOW?

Treasure Island lies off the coast of Melemele Island. It's a wild Pokémon reserve, with no humans living there.

PIKACHU VALLEY

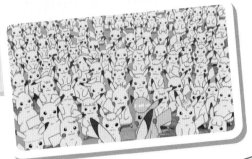

Pikachu Valley is home to a group of Pikachu. They live in a Pikachu shaped trailer and their Trainer, Pikala, is a Pikachu super-fan!

DOS & DON'TS
OF . . . PIKACHU VALLEY

Do wear your favorite Pikachu ears and tail to fit in.

Don't wait around for Pikala to do a roll call of the Pikachu—you will be there for hours!

Do add "Pika" to everything you say!

Don't upset a Pikachu nicknamed the Boss, he might challenge you to a battle.

BEWEAR'S DEN

A very special Pokémon environment is Bewear's den, deep in the forest on Melemele Island. Here Bewear looks after Stufful, the pre-evolved form of Bewear. Bewear and Stufful provide lavish feasts of fruit and a cozy nest to sleep in for their guests, Team Rocket.

Who's Who?

Molayne
The cousin of Ash's pal Sophocles, Molayne works at Hokulani Observatory. He is helping the world to understand unusual Pokémon from space.

Molayne

Pikala
This cheerful guide works at Pikachu Valley, on Akala Island. She is also a keen Pokémon Trainer.

Pikala

AKALA ISLAND

With a skyline dominated by a smoldering volcano, this island is famous for its Fire Festival, Wela Volcano Park, and also its wrestling events. Its people are passionate about everything they do.

DID YOU KNOW?

The superstar wrestler of the region, the Masked Royal, always partners with Incineroar, a Fire- and Dark-type Pokémon. His catchphrase is "Enjoy!"

DON'T MISS: POKÉMON PARADISE RESORT

- The Pokémon spa features **hot springs** and a **flower bath**.

- There is a care area offering **counseling**, **fatigue recovery**, and **moisturising**.

- Metal Pokémon, like Metang, can enjoy a **scented oil massage**.

- For pure pleasure, there are the **biggest flume rides** you have ever seen!

Who's Who?

Kiawe
Ash's fellow student at the Pokémon School, Kiawe is a top Trainer with a faithful Charizard. He also helps on the family farm every day. His temperament is either super-calm or super-excited!

Olivia
The Kahuna of Akala Island, Olivia likes to share its culture with others, encouraging visitors to explore the island by sending them on a quest to source ingredients for Akala curry.

Kiawe

TOP FESTIVALS

The Wela Fire Festival

Time your visit to this island to coincide with the Wela Fire Festival, celebrating the island's volcano and fiery spirit. Here the Kahuna will present the most impressive Pokémon with the coveted Volcano Crown.

TASTY FOODS
MOOMOO MARVELS

Creamy milk and delicious ice-cream are specialties of the island, thanks to its rich, volcanic soil that produces lush grass for Miltank to graze on. The dairy products are delivered all over the Alola region by Pelipper and the occasional Charizard.

FUN SPORTS

Battle Dome Battle Royal

No visitor to Akala Island should miss a Battle Royal match at the Battle Dome. Here top wrestlers match their skills—and if they are the Revengers, maybe cheat a bit! The Double Royals made their debut here, with Ash Royal joining the Masked Royal in a tag team.

PONI ISLAND

The site of the famous Altar of the Sunne, Poni Island is where all four Island Guardians come together in a time of crisis. This magical island is a place of enchantment and life-changing experiences.

TASTY FOODS
RAVISHING RADISHES

Poni Island radishes are a crunchy treat loved all over the Alola region. Grown here by the Kahuna, Hapu, the radishes are delicate and must be harvested carefully. Although delicious in many recipes, Hapu recommends just eating them on their own while fresh.

TOP 3 MUST SEES

1. Altar of the Sunne
This spectacular ruin was once the site of a battle between the Island Deities and the Ultra Beasts. Ancient murals here depict the legend of the Blinding One who brought light to the region.

2. Poni Canyon
A vast rocky valley, Poni Canyon leads to the Altar of the Sunne. Riddled with mysterious caves, it contains a magnetic field that helps Charjabug evolve.

3. The Ruins of Hope
This ancient temple on the coast is filled with beautiful coral and colorful seaweed. Here one can sometimes meet Island Guardian Tapu Fini.

DON'T MISS:
VIKAVOLT VOOM

- This **annual race** brings competitors from all over the Alola region.

- Vikavolt Trainers use a **virtual reality headset** to lead their Pokémon across a mixed-terrain course.

- The race is hosted by **Anna**, a popular TV presenter and commentator.

NEED TO KNOW:
SEAFOLK VILLAGE

- Seafolk Village is home to the **Seafolk**, a group of people that travel the world's many oceans.

- Ash's Seafolk friends Ida and Kanoa travel in a **Steelix-shaped houseboat**.

- From Seafolk Village port you can catch a boat to **Melemele Island** and other places too.

EVOLUTION SOLUTION

Beware of these Pokémon guarding the way to the Altar of the Sunne! Jangmo-o and its Evolutions Hakamo-o and Kommo-o are Scaly Pokémon with tough head scales. Hakamo-o displays its scars to show its prowess, while Kommo-o clatters its tail scales to frighten opponents.

Jangmo-o

Hakamo-o

Kommo-o

AETHER PARADISE

This futuristic man-made island is home to the Aether Foundation—a scientific research project dedicated to protecting Pokémon. Secretly, it is trying to find out why Ultra Beasts come to the Alola region, and how to combat them.

DID YOU KNOW?

The awesome Manalo Stadium, another man-made island, is located near Aether Paradise. Both benefit from the generally idyllic sea conditions in the area.

What to Pack

Beast Balls—Bring these Poké Balls to catch powerful Ultra Beasts and protect the Alola region.

Medical kit—Battling Ultra Beasts is dangerous work. Take some berries with healing properties and medicine for the journey.

Matching uniforms—So everyone knows you are a part of the Ultra Guardian team!

Beast Balls

Medical kit

NEED TO KNOW:
ULTRA GUARDIANS

- The Aether Foundation created the Ultra Guardian task force to tackle **Ultra Beast emergencies**.

- Ash and his fellow students use a secret **Ultra Base** under the Pokémon school.

- They have **cool uniforms** and use **Beast Balls** to catch their Ultra Beast foes.

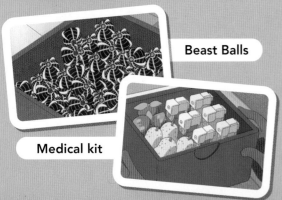

Who's Who?

Lusamine
The head of the Aether Foundation, Lusamine is totally dedicated to her work and has little time for family. She is the mother of Ash's friend Lillie, who she embarrasses by calling her "baby girl."

Faba
This ambitious scientist is prepared to put others at risk to further his research. He is a Trainer of Psychic-type Pokémon and inventor of devices that go wrong.

Professor Burnet
This researcher of Ultra Wormholes is vital to the work of the Foundation. She is married to Professor Kukui.

Wicke
Wicke is a top scientist who always has time for students and loves to give tours of the labs. She is vice chief of the Aether Foundation.

Lusamine

Faba

Professor Burnet

Wicke

SPOT THAT POKÉMON

In the Aether Paradise's conservation area look out for Ditto, who can imitate other Pokémon. Type: Null was developed in the labs here and evolved to become Silvally, while Clefable helps run the base of the Ultra Guardians.

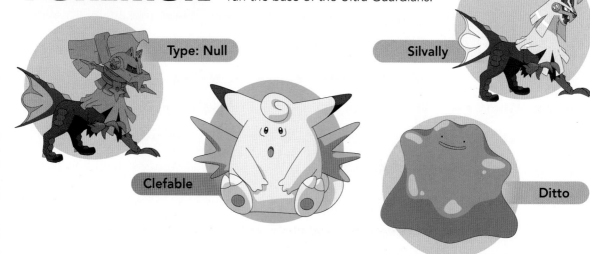

Type: Null

Silvally

Clefable

Ditto

ULTRA SPACE

Just a wormhole away is the realm of the Ultra Beasts. It appears dark and desolate because it has been robbed of vital energy by an ancient disaster. Its weird and wonderful locations are home to the strangest Pokémon.

Poipole

SPOT THAT POKÉMON

This unearthly realm is home to many Ultra Beasts—some terrifying, some enchanting. Nihilego wanted to control Lusamine and kidnapped her. Poipole, full of pranks, became Ash's friend. Naganadel, the Evolution of Poipole, could speak and revealed many secrets of this realm.

Who's Who?

Dia
Once an Ultra Ranger, Dia quit because he refused to flee from the Ultra Beast Guzzlord. He teams up with Ash and Tapu Koko to save the day.

Zeraora
This Thunderclap Pokémon is Dia's loyal ally. Among its many attacks are Close Combat and Plasma Fist. Don't touch its tail—you might get a shock!

Dia and Zeraora

Nihilego

Naganadel

TOP 3 ULTRA MUST SEES

1. Ultra Deep Sea
This twilight expanse of floating rocks and drifting UB Symbionts is an awe-inspiring sight. If you ever visit, beware—a Symbiont might try to bond with you, turning you into its puppet!

2. Poipole's World
A bleak landscape of deep rocky chasms and dark caves, Poipole's world was once a fertile paradise of flowers and light.

3. Ultra Ruins
In a parallel world, the Ultra Beast Guzzlord has reduced Hau'oli City to Ultra Ruins! Here, even the Pokémon School is rubble.

DID YOU KNOW?

Ultra Beasts travel to the Alola region by creating Ultra Wormholes—holes in space itself. The Aether Foundation has created the technology to make their own and send the Beasts home!

1

2

3

What to Pack

Backpack and supplies—Food for Pokémon and Trainers is scarce in this realm.

Your Z-Ring—If a parallel-world Island Deity appears, you might just be able to use it.

Warm clothes—There are few comforts here. If you have to stay overnight, you could be sleeping in the wild.

Top Tip!

There is still much more of Ultra Space to explore! Solgaleo and Ash went on an adventure and saw new places and Ultra Beasts!

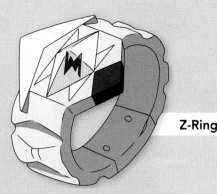

Z-Ring

ALOLA REGION ATTRACTIONS

From the moment you arrive in the Alola region you know
it's a special place where they do things their own way!
Here are just a few of the things that make it so unique.

TOP 3 MUST PLAY

1. Pokébase
  Pokébase, or Pokémon baseball, is popular
  in the Alola region. Catch a pro-league
  match, or better still join in a friendly game.

2. Catch Adventure Race
  Why not enter this fast paced race?
  Be the fastest to get across an island
  while catching specific Pokémon at
  each of the three checkpoints.

3. Pokémon Ping-pong
  If you like indoor sports then try your hand
  at Pokémon Ping-pong. Your Pokémon can
  use moves to return the ball!

Top Tip!

Another attraction
of the Alola region is its Island
Trial system. Instead of fighting
Trainers in Gym battles, you face
a wise Kahuna who will test your
mettle. Even if you lose,
you often gain a mentor
and friend.

NEED TO KNOW: Z-MOVE MAYHEM

- Are you a fan of Pokémon battles?
  Then visit the Alola region to see
  awesome Z-Moves in action.

- Wearing a **Z-Ring**, a Trainer has the
  chance to become one with their Pokémon
  and unleash incredible new powers.

- Z-Rings house powerful **Z-Crystals**,
  which are needed to perform Z-Moves.

DON'T MISS:
RIDE POKÉMON

- Have you ever wanted to **ride a Pelipper** or **Lapras**? Then the Alola region is the place for you.

- Here, it's customary to board a Ride Pokémon to **travel over terrain quickly**.

- On the island of Akala, visitors can ride **Stoutland** to get about. From Hau'oli City, **Mantine** will take you surfing across the waves to visit Treasure Island!

DID YOU KNOW?

The Ultra Guardians use Ride Pokémon to travel into other dimensions. Ash rides Garchomp, Sophocles has Metang, and Lillie uses Altaria.

PIKACHU'S TOP Z-MOVES

Gigavolt Havoc

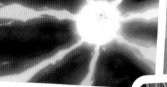

Volt Thunderbolt

Corkscrew Crash

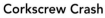

MYSTICAL RUINS

The islands of the Alola region all have one intriguing feature—ancient ruins. These sites may be old, but they are not abandoned. Island Guardians, Kahunas, and those facing Island Trials can all be seen in these unique places.

What to Pack

A torch—Many of these sites have dark caves, tunnels, and hidden shrines.

Your water bottle and sun protection—Finding these ruins will take a good walk, usually in hot conditions.

A sense of humor—The Island Guardians like to prank and play, so be prepared to smile as well as battle!

THE RUINS OF ABUNDANCE

Found on Ula'ula, these ruins celebrate the fertility of the region. Here, Tapu Bulu can make trees grow and blossom in seconds, fruit appear from nowhere, and a grassy field cover the barren rocks.

Tapu Bulu

THE RUINS OF HOPE

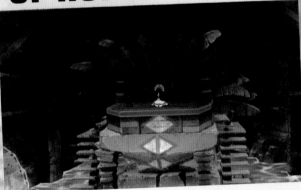

Poni Island is an enchanting seaside location for these ruins. The ruins are visible at low tide but underwater at high tide, set in a crystal pool of sunlit sea. The Island Deity, Tapu Fini, can be found on Poni Island.

Tapu Fini

THE RUINS OF LIFE

These ruins are in a beautiful jungle location on Akala Island. There are overgrown monuments, crumbling stone stairways, and a candlelit altar to Tapu Lele.

Tapu Lele

THE RUINS OF CONFLICT

Tapu Koko can be found in these rocky ruins on Melemele Island. The Island Deity can bless Trainers and Kahuna Hala ahead of a grand trial battle.

Tapu Koko

TOP FESTIVALS

Manalo Festival
The ruins of the Alola region play a big role in the Manalo Festival, which occurs once every 21 years during the solar eclipse. Each Island Kahuna visits their respective island's ruins to offer thanks to the Blinding One, the Legendary Pokémon said to have created the Alola region.

Kahuna Hapu sees a spirit at the Ruins of Hope

DOS & DON'TS
OF . . . SACRED SITES

Do visit if you wish to honor an Island Deity. They welcome all those with respect in their hearts.

Don't battle here without permission— you will anger a Guardian, who may punish you!

Do bring your Pokémon here if they are tired or injured. These are powerful places of healing.

Don't be surprised if you witness something magical! Spirits, transformations, and weird powers can often be seen in these sites!

LEGENDARY AND MYTHICAL

The sunny, fertile land of the Alola region has produced many unique Pokémon. Its special connection to another dimension has also attracted Ultra Beasts—and the Legendary Pokémon that battle them.

Lunala

Type: Psychic-Ghost
Height: 13 ft 1 in (4 m)
This Moone Pokémon is said to be created from the moon itself. It unites with Solgaleo to help restore harmony to the universe. It can create Ultra Wormholes to travel through.

Poipole

Type: Poison
Height: 2 ft (0.6 m)
This Poison Pin Pokémon at first seems fond of naughty pranks. Ash and Pikachu befriend it and learned that it had been sent from the realm of the Ultra Beasts to seek help.

Solgaleo

Type: Psychic-Steel
Height: 11 ft 2 in (3.4 m)
Myths say this Pokémon is the sun made flesh. It is one of the Legendary Pokémon that is said to have fought the Ultra Beasts at the Altar of the Sunne to save the Alola region in years gone by.

Type: Null

Type: Normal

Height: 6 ft 3 in (1.9 m)

Type: Null can sense Ultra Beasts and Ultra Wormholes. The mask on its face limits its power in order to keep it under control. It can evolve into the Pokémon Silvally.

Marshadow

Type: Fighting-Ghost

Height: 2 ft 4 in (0.7 m)

This mysterious Pokémon can slip into others' shadows and mimic their powers and movements. The Gloomdweller Pokémon can become even stronger than those it's imitating.

Magearna

Type: Steel-Fairy

Height: 3 ft 3 in (1 m)

Magearna is great at looking after others. This Pokémon can synchronize its consciousness with people and Pokémon to understand their feelings.

Necrozma

Type: Psychic

Height: 7 ft 10 in (2.4 m)

A Prism Pokémon once known as the Blinding One, Necrozma's power brought life and light to the Alola region. Necrozma was viewed as a threat, until it was discovered by the Ultra Guardians to be a vital ally.

DID YOU KNOW?

Lillie's Magearna, the Artificial Pokémon, was bought by her father, Mohn, when in need of repair. Now active again, Magearna helped Lillie and her family search for the lost Mohn.

FESTIVAL FUN

Thinking of a vacation in the Alola region? You could build a holiday around one of their colorful festivals or amazing sporting events. Just take a look at everything that's going on!

TOP FESTIVALS

The Bread Festival

Will you rise to the challenge in the Alola Bread Festival? Anyone can enter this celebration of Alola's many types of bread. The best baker wins a luxury cruise! Mallow's family restaurant, Aina's Kitchen, once won top prize with Jelly Bread.

FUN SPORTS

Finals Frenzy

For the ultimate sports holiday, why not watch the Alola Pokémon League finals at the Manalo Stadium? The top 16 players face a Battle Royal, then it's a knock-out format to the grand final! Ash won the inaugural event. The floating stadium alone is worth the trip —with restaurants and shops galore.

DOS & DON'TS
OF . . . THE POKÉMON PANCAKE RACE

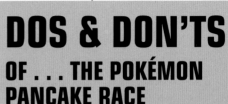

Do bring your Pokémon. They will have to race with you.

Don't let your Pokémon use any attacks on opponents—they will be disqualified.

Do remember you must pull your Pokémon in a cart. So a Pikachu will be easier than a Snorlax!

Don't forget to have a pancake on the day— honey and berries with ice-cream is a favorite.

REVIEW:
MALIE CITY

Every day is like a festival at Malie City on Ula'ula Island! The building design and clothes style are inspired by the Johto region, which is so cool! Even the tour guides dress as ninjas, and tourists can borrow traditional clothing for the day, too. The most exciting part is Malie Garden and the working Pokémon. Pokémon like Passimian and Hariyama work at the gardens transporting visitors around, while Floslass serves up tasty food and drinks in the cafés. Make sure to check out the observation deck—you can see the whole garden from there, including the beautiful bridges and fountains.

DID YOU KNOW?

In Malie City you can try delicious breakfast balls served on sticks —an island specialty— with secret spicy sauce.

GALAR REGION

Misty forests, mysterious stone ruins, and ancient myths abound in this great island. It is full of surprises, like the fact that its Pokémon can Dynamax—grow to giant size! This sports-filled land is also the place to watch the World Coronation Series.

WYNDON CITY

Wyndon City, in the northern Galar region, is home to the massive Pokémon dueling arena of Wyndon Stadium. It is a bustling historic city of museums, red buses, and leafy parks. It is also the transport hub to the Wild Area and beyond.

TASTY FOODS
SWEET SCONES

Among the top treats of the Galar region are scones, super-sweet little cakes that are usually enjoyed with a cup of milk tea. They make a handy takeaway, but be careful—a cheeky Skwovet might take yours away from you!

What to Pack

Hoody, sunglasses, and rain hat— In case its cool, or it's hot, or in case it pours ... be prepared for all weathers in this ever-changing land.

Tickets for a big match at Wyndon Stadium—You can't miss the spectacle of a Dynamax-style Pokémon duel!

Your autograph book— Imagine bumping into a stellar Pokémon champion like Leon and missing the opportunity!

Wyndon Stadium

TRAINER TIPS

- Contenders can fight their way up the ranks to become one of the Masters Eight, then fight to become "Monarch"—the champion!

- Leon is the current Monarch. He is on a long winning streak and called "unbeatable." While ruthless in a duel, he has a kind personality, giving Ash a friendly unofficial duel when he requests it.

Leon

TOP 3 MUST SEES

1. Wyndon Station
This is one of the first stops for Pokémon Trainers visiting the Galar region. From this huge station you can get buses and trains all over the region.

2. Rose Tower
This huge tower in Wyndon City belongs to businessman Chairman Rose. He is the owner of Macros Cosmos, a powerful organization in the Galar region.

3. Motostoke Riverbank
Near Wyndon City is the beautiful Wild Area of Motostoke Riverbank. Wild Pokémon like Gossifleur love to play by the riverside under the aqueduct.

SPOT THAT POKÉMON

In Wyndon there are top fighting Pokémon at the stadium. You can see Charizard and Gyarados, plus quaint local Pokémon in the parks and alleyways, like the hungry Skwovet and Nickit. Watch out for rampaging Drednaw, which can Dynamax to the size of a building!

Nickit

Drednaw

Skwovet

DOS & DON'TS
WITH . . . SCORBUNNY

Do look out for Scorbunny when you are in the Galar region. This Rabbit Pokémon is full of tricks.

Don't leave your scones and other snacks unattended. Scorbunny might run off with them!

Do take time to appreciate Scorbunny's soccer skills. It is a master of fancy footwork!

Don't judge this Pokémon too quickly. It will only steal your food to help other, starving Pokémon, like Nickit.

Scorbunny

THE WILD AREA

Prepare to be dazzled by the rare beauty of the Galar region's Wild Area. Sitting far beyond the noise of the city, it's a wonderful wilderness filled with Pokémon. You can find diverse habitats rich in variety: grasslands, desert, forests, and mountains.

GETTING THERE

1. **Taking the train**
   To reach the Wild Area, take a train from Wyndon. You may need to wait a while—the services can be patchy!

2. **Taking the bus**
   A bus network is also available. These can be less frequent than the trains!

3. **A long hike**
   Once in the area, be prepared to hike to your final destination. Bring walking boots and a backpack. Your Rotom Phone will provide maps and routes.

Who's Who?

Bray Zenn

Bray Zenn
This fossil scientist can be found working hard in remote spots, discovering ancient Pokémon and recreating them with his Fossil Restore Machine. He loves to argue with his colleague, Cara Liss.

Cara Liss
Cara is a top fossil expert and works for the Pewter Museum. She is full of theories and can describe a whole fossil and its original way of life just from seeing a few bones. She is quite forgetful and laid-back.

Cara Liss

SPOT THAT POKÉMON

Out in this great wilderness you can find Boldore and Wooloo in the fields, and Maractus blooming with their colorful flowers. In the sunshine spot Butterfree fluttering by and Flygon soaring free.

A WILD CURRY

The Galar region is known for its many types of curry. In the Wild Area it's the perfect campfire meal, heartwarming and fun to make. It's full of freshly picked ingredients like Pecha Berry and Micle Berry.

Boldore

Wooloo

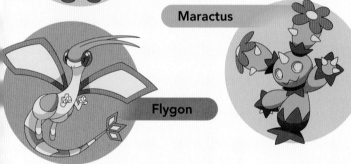

Maractus

Flygon

Butterfree

DOS & DON'TS
OF . . . FOSSIL HUNTING

Do bring a Fossil Restore Machine—it will connect and reanimate jumbled old bones.

Do bring your camping gear—you will need to reach some remote locations far from a convenient hotel.

Don't restore fossils if you can't control them! Dracovish and Arctozolt are quite a handful!

Don't misjudge fossil Pokémon. A Dracovish on the rampage might only be looking for a place to swim!

Cara revives Dracovish using the Fossil Restore Machine

UNIQUE POKÉMON ENVIRONMENTS

The Galar region has a rich diversity of Pokémon environments, including historic coal-mining regions, rolling fields, and remote islands. Every location attracts its own special Pokémon.

DYNAMAX POKÉMON

The Galar region provides an unique environment for amazing Dynamax and Gigantamax Pokémon to appear. These giant temporary transformations are caused by mysterious Galar Particles. Trainers need powerful Dynamax Bands to control Pokémon in this state.

TOP 3 MUST SEES

1. Snorlax
Watch out for a Dynamaxed Snorlax—it becomes a whole hillside, with trees growing on top!

2. Centiskorch
Another unmissable sight is a Gigantamax Centiskorch. The Radiator Pokémon can grow as long as an express train—but stand well back from its two-thousand degree heat!

3. Drednaw
In Wyndon, you might spot a Gigantamax Drednaw. Watch from a safe distance—they have a very powerful chomp.

FIELDS OF GREEN

With plenty of rainfall, the Galar region is a lush land. Tympole sing in the streams, and Goomy crawl among the bushes. In the woodlands, watch out for Grubbin dangling from the branches and Phantump among the leaves.

Goomy

Tympole

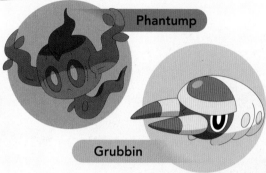

Phantump

Grubbin

MINES

In the Galar region, you can find working mines among the rolling hills. These mines can draw in the Pokémon Coalossal. Beware of the heat—Coalossal's stomach is a giant furnace! The miners don't always enjoy having Coalossal nearby, especially when one Dynamaxes and goes on a rampage.

Coalossal

Carkol

EVOLUTION SOLUTION

Rolycoly

Coalossal is the final Evolution of the Coal Pokémon. It can begin life as Rolycoly, a Pokémon which was first found in a coal mine about 400 years ago; then evolves into Carkol before finally becoming the massive Coalossal.

DID YOU KNOW?

The miners are doing work for the energy plant under Hammerlocke Stadium owned by Macro Cosmos.

WEDGEHURST

This sleepy town in the south of the Galar region has a picturesque beauty, with a gentle river running through it. But don't let its sweet looks fool you—Wedgehurst is a vital center of Pokémon research and the study of Dynamaxing.

Sonia

Who's Who?

Sonia
With a lively mind and outgoing nature, Sonia is studying to be a Pokémon professor. She has been Leon's friend since childhood, and they both grew up loving Pokémon. Her motto is "I refuse to lose!"

Professor Magnolia
A brilliant scientist, Professor Magnolia is Sonia's grandma. She has spent her life studying the effects of Galar Particles, and helped Chairman Rose create the Dynamax Band to harness their power.

DON'T MISS:
THE CENTER OF MYSTERY

- Wedgehurst is home to a **Pokémon Research Lab**, run by Professor Magnolia.

- With its **distinctive spire** it looks like a cozy cottage, but houses the latest high-tech equipment.

- All the facilities exist here to create important **Dynamax Bands** for Pokémon Trainers.

Professor Magnolia

DID YOU KNOW?

Wishing Stars are also studied at Wedgehurst. These glowing rocks fall from the sky across the Galar region. Professor Magnolia discovered they contain particles that cause Pokémon to grow to giant size.

NEED TO KNOW:
GETTING AROUND

- While Wedgehurst does have a **station**, your own set of wheels can be useful to reach historic sites.

- A familiar sight in the area is **Sonia's pink car**, a vintage vehicle that she drives with a wild style all of her own. Ask Ash's friend Goh, who has been her passenger!

Gigantamax Machamp

TRAINER TIPS

- In the Galar region a Dynamax Band is vital for Pokémon Trainers to harness the power of their Pokémon.

- The band enables the Pokémon to use special Dynamax moves like Max Lightning and Max Airstream, which are epic in battle.

- The band can also make a Pokémon attain its Gigantamax form, usually involving a dramatic change of appearance.

Glowing Dynamax Band

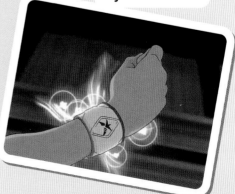

STOW-ON-SIDE

Stow-on-Side is known for its ancient mural and two Pokémon gyms. Nearby, nestled among gently rolling countryside, is the town of Turffield. Inhabited since ancient times, it contains many historic stones and mysterious ruins.

DID YOU KNOW?

Some experts connect the Turffield Geoglyph with an old Galar region legend about gigantic Pokémon that once terrorized the land. In those tales, a young hero with a sword and shield saved the day!

Who's Who?

Bea
Bea is the confident Gym Leader of the massive Stow-on-Side Stadium. She was trained in Galar karate by her father, and specializes in Fighting-type Pokémon.

Bea

Allister
Shy Allister is the Gym Leader of a Ghost-type Pokémon Gym. He is very close to his Ghost-type Pokémon, and can even speak to them!

Allister

Top Tip!

Allister can help Ghost-type Pokémon like Gengar to Gigantamax by making a special mushroom soup.

TOP 3 MUST SEES

1. The Turffield Geoglyph
A stone image set in the ground, this mysterious ruin has fascinated people for many years.

2. Ghost Train
Catch the spooky Ghost Train from Wyndon Station to Stow-on-Side. Usually only Ghost-type Pokémon catch this locomotive, but Allister sometimes hops on board.

3. The Stow-On-Side Mural
This nearby ancient mural conceals hidden statues, which show Pokémon holding a sword and shield —another part of the old legends.

Vortex next to Dynamax Pangoro

NEED TO KNOW: VORTEX SYMBOLS

- Visitors are fascinated by the symbol of a vortex, a key part of the **geoglyph**. The tail of the vortex points to the giant Pokémon.

- The symbol is significant in the Galar region, as a giant black vortex is said to have appeared on the **mythical Darkest Day**, when the land faced destruction.

- Vortexes are often associated with the appearance of a giant Pokémon of some kind. So the ancient symbol could shed light on the Galar region's **Dynamax phenomenon**.

SPOT THAT POKÉMON

Ghost-type Pokémon can be spotted in the forest near Stow-on-Side, like stone looking Galarian Corsola and the Elder Tree Pokémon Trevenant.

Galarian Corsola

Trevenant

THE SLUMBERING WEALD

There are many intriguing places in the enchanted region of Galar, but none quite so steeped in mystery as the Slumbering Weald. This area of ancient forest has some very rare Pokémon indeed.

Top Tip!

Don't be afraid if the Warrior Pokémon in the forest seem to leap at you. They won't hurt you, and just fade away into thin air.

Shield and sword appearing in the weald

TYPICAL WEATHER

If there is one kind of weather this location is famous for, it is fog! A thick mist can roll across the weald at any time. This weather phenomenon can cause trains to be stopped and visitors to get seriously lost!

NEED TO KNOW:
MYTHICAL MARVELS

- The Slumbering Weald has special powers. It can send you into a **gentle slumber** with its enchanted mist.

- An **overgrown temple** lies in the depths of the forest. This is where Legendary Pokémon will heed a call to help.

- Watch out for the **ancient relics**, an old sword and shield. Found in the forest they can transform into Zacian and Zamazenta.

SPOT THAT POKÉMON

The Slumbering Weald is the place to spot Zacian and Zamazanta, the Warrior Pokémon that defend the Galar region. They defeated Eternatus when the Darkest Day came.

Zacian

Zamazenta

Eternatus

Bunnelby

DOS & DON'TS

OF . . . THE WEALD

Do search for Bunnelby! The Pokémon with the amazing digging ears can be found here.

Don't expect to catch the Warrior Pokémon Zacian and Zamazenta here. They have a special purpose, to protect the Galar region and remain free spirits.

Do look out for Galar Particles falling from the sky. This bright red display is common in the area, and is a wonderful sight.

Don't wander too far if your train is delayed by fog and they open the doors. It might just start up again quickly and leave you behind!

THE GLIMWOOD TANGLE

One of the most curious places in the Galar region is the Glimwood Tangle, a magical forest famous in storybooks. Visits to this enchanted place can seem like a dream. The Glimwood Tangle is a mystery and offers unique encounters with Pokémon.

DID YOU KNOW?

Impidimp are the pranksters of the forest, and love to play tricks—or start a food fight with mushy berries! Play along and they can soon prove to be friendly and helpful.

TOP 3 MUST SEES

1. The Luminous Mushrooms
Among the most magical forest spectacles, the glowing mushrooms come in a variety of colors and giant sizes. They light your way in the dark.

2. Ballonlea
Deep in the woods, a wanderer may stumble upon the pretty town Ballonlea, full of quaint cottages and fantastical fungi. It is a safe haven for the lost and a good place to stop for a rest.

3. The Green Ravine
An emerald light falls in this wonderful grotto of spreading ferns and pretty mosses. But be careful not to fall down it, like Rapidash!

SPOT THAT POKÉMON

The Galarian forms of Ponyta and Rapidash are one of the attractions of the forest. Instead of fiery manes, they have beautiful flowing hair of purple and aqua. Meanwhile Alcremie, the Cream Pokémon, are essential for the Ballonlea cake decorating contest.

Galarian Ponyta

Alcremie

Galarian Rapidash

Morelull

TOP FESTIVALS

All-Alcremie Decoration Challenge
Ballonlea Gym Leader Opal hosts a unusual cake decorating contest in the small forest town. Contestants have to use the Pokémon Alcremie to make and decorate cakes. The Trainer and Pokémon with the tastiest and prettiest cake wins a battle with Opal! Be careful not to eat too much while decorating, or you might be too full to battle!

NEED TO KNOW:
FOREST MYSTERIES

- **Gentle rain** falls here—even when you seem totally sheltered by enormous trees!

- Morelull live here, and other **Pokémon snack on the tasty cups** that sprout from their heads!

- If you read a story about this place, its **characters can appear** to you and call you on a fantasy-like adventure.

HAMMERLOCKE CITY

In the center of the Galar region, Hammerlocke is a powerhouse of fuel production and technology. It is also a city of sport, with a vast stadium for Pokémon battles. The city has seen incredible events that have shaped the destiny of the region.

Top Tip!

The summit of Hammerlocke Tower has a great view—it is also the perfect place for a legendary battle!

Gigantic Eternatus

Who's Who?

Chairman Rose
President of Macro Cosmos, Chairman Rose has risen from humble beginnings. His dream is to provide the region with power, no matter what the risks.

Oleana
The assistant of Chairman Rose, Oleana will do anything to support his plans. Her ice-cool exterior hides a fiery anger when she doesn't get her way.

Chairman Rose

Oleana

NEED TO KNOW:
THE DARKEST DAY

- **Historic events** rocked this city when the Pokémon known as the Darkest Day was revived by Chairman Rose due to its great power.

- The Gigantic Pokémon was named **Eternatus**.

- Out of control, it had to be defeated by Legendary Pokémon **Zacian** and **Zamazenta**—with help from Ash and Goh.

DON'T MISS:
HAMMERLOCKE TOWER

- If dining in Hammerlocke, make sure to visit the **restaurant** in Hammerlocke Tower.

- It is famous for its **spectacular views** over the glittering city at night.

- It serves **gourmet food**, from specialty salads to sweet treats. Humans and Pokémon will not be disappointed!

- Hammerlocke Tower also has **luxury hotel rooms** for guests.

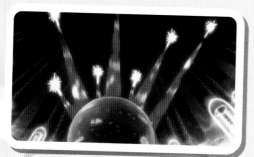

DID YOU KNOW?

Another feature of Hammerlocke City is its underground power plant, which once used the Pokémon Eternatus to generate energy for the city. Overloads sent Galar Particles into the sky, causing Pokémon to Dynamax across the land!

TRAINER TIPS

- The Hammerlocke Gym is famous throughout the Galar region. It's all thanks to the sponsorship of Chairman Rose.

- Raihan is the Hammerlocke Gym Leader. He ranks highly in the World Coronation Series and often uses Duraludon in battle.

- Dragon-type Pokémon are the specialty of the Gym.

- The current Monarch of the World Coronation series, Leon, also trains there.

Leon at the Hammerlocke Gym gate

COASTAL GALAR

The Galar region has many sandy beaches and beautiful seaside towns. They are not only a great place for a holiday, but they also offer a chance to see unique Pokémon. As well as the fascinating local Pokémon variants, you might receive a rare Eiscue visitor by sea.

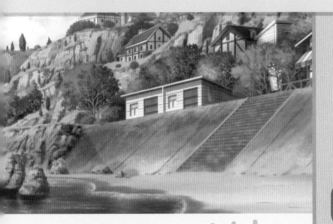

TASTY FOODS
EISCUE ICE-CREAM

For a traditional seaside treat, why not have a cone from the ice-cream cart right by the beach? Pecha Berry is a popular flavor. But you might have to wait your turn if a wandering Eiscue is dipping its head in the freezer!

TOP 3 MUST SEES

1. Green Woodland
There is beautiful scenery just inland from the coast. Take a stroll by the meandering river, among moss-covered old walls surrounded by lush woodland.

2. Icy Islands
Take a boat trip to see the remote beauty of the nearby Eiscue Islands and their spectacular ice floes.

3. High Waterfall
The tall waterfall just off the coast is a must see—but avoid if you are kayaking or canoeing, of course!

SPOT THAT POKÉMON

In this area you can see Wingull flying in the sky and region-specific Pokémon like Galarian Stunfisk, which hide in the mud waiting for their prey. If you are lucky you might spot Eiscue, which occasionally float over on an iceberg from their snowy home.

Galarian Stunfisk

Eiscue

Wingull

Falinks

DOS & DON'TS

WITH . . . FALINKS

Do try to see Falinks if you are in the Galar region. The Formation Pokémon is made of a brass—the leader—and five troopers.

Don't expect every Falinks to be perfect in its teamwork. Like everything, its skills take practice.

Do try and see one in battle. Here, their sense of organization can turn them into an unstoppable battering ram.

Don't be afraid to help out if a brass needs some training. Show it the way and it can be a quick learner.

Top Tip!

If fighting Falinks, separate the brass from the troopers to create confusion. But beware, Pikachu once did this and the troopers adopted it as the leader!

LEGENDARY AND MYTHICAL

From fierce Fighting-type Pokémon to brave heroes, this historic land is home to Legendary and Mythical Pokémon of earth-shaking power.

Zamazenta
Type: Fighting
Height: 9 ft 6 in (2.9 m)
When Zamazenta is in its Crowned Shield form it can defend against powerful attacks, including those of Dynamax Pokémon.

Kubfu
Type: Fighting
Height: 2 ft (0.6 m)
Kubfu can increase its fighting spirit by pulling the white hair on its head.

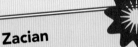

Zacian
Type: Fairy
Height: 9 ft 2 in (2.8 m)
The Galar region's very own legendary hero has triumphed in many battles. Zacian can absorb metal particles which are then transformed into weapons.

Urshifu
Type: Fighting-Dark
Height: 6 ft 3 in (1.9 m)
The Wushu Pokémon mainly lives in the mountains, practicing its fighting moves on the sheer cliffs. It is the Evolution of Kubfu.

Zarude

Type: Dark-Grass

Height: 5 ft 11 in (1.8 m)

This intimidating Rogue Monkey Pokémon lives in packs within dense forests.

Eternatus

Type: Poison-Dragon

Height: 65 ft 7 in (20 m)

This Gigantic Pokémon was once known as the Darkest Day, as its power almost destroyed the Galar region. It has now been caught by Goh and Ash and is kept in a secret location.

GALARIAN GETAWAYS

Fancy a truly unique vacation? Somewhere that combines ancient history, fantasy, and the tastiest food? The only place you can see Pokémon Dynamax? Go to the Galar region for a truly great experience!

FOOD TOUR

Seeing all the magnificent sites of the Galar region can be tiring, so be sure to take time out and stop for refreshment at one of the regions's cafés and restaurants.

1. Traditional Tea Bar
Try a Galarian specialty of Moomoo milk at the traditional tea bars in Wyndon City. And don't forget the scones, of course!

2. Galarian Trains
Enjoy a tasty lunch with a stunning view while traveling through the Galar region. The catering carriage has waiters serving a variety of food.

3. Ballonlea Patisserie
At the Ballonlea Patisserie you can buy scrumptious cupcakes and other sweets. The secret to the delicious taste is the cream, made by the Pokémon Alcremie.

FLAVOR FRENZY!

The Galar region is all about curry, and you can find it just about anywhere! Don't worry if your meals start to disappear in front of your eyes. It might be Sobble trying to join in the fun. Water makes it invisible —and curry makes it hungry!

Gigantamax curry and boiled egg curry

Plenty of potato curry and tropical curry

REVIEW:
THE TALE OF YOU AND GLIMWOOD TANGLE

When in the Galar region you must read this amazing fantasy, set in a magical forest.

The characters are so real they seem to come to life—in fact, sometimes they do come to life and take you into their realm!

DON'T MISS:
POKÉMON CENTER SERVICES

- The Galar region's dedicated Pokémon Centers will take care of you and your Pokémon's needs —including **providing food** if they are hungry!

- Been in a duel? Any Center will give your Pokémon the **rest and care** they need to return to fighting form.

- Puzzled about the Galar region Pokémon? **Nurse Joy** will be happy to educate you with key facts.

- Need extra help? Highly intelligent **Indeedee** are always on hand, and the female Indeedee make excellent babysitters.

Male Indeedee

Female Indeedee

CUSTOMER REVIEW:
"THIS IS THE BEST I'VE EVER TASTED"

Leek curry

Whipped cream curry

TEAM ROCKET: GALAR REGION

Prepare for trouble—and make it double!

Welcome to the Team Rocket's guide to misadventures in the Galar region!

Prize Master

What to Pack

A Secret Team Rocket Prize Master—This machine, delivered by Pelipper, will dispense Pokémon from out of a clear blue sky.

A Rotom Phone—To identify powerful and rare Pokémon to capture.

Sunglasses—To hide your identity, of course!

GETTING AROUND

Here's some Team Rocket travel expertise! Don't rattle around the Galar region in a train, like a boring twerp! Why not float in style in a hot-air balloon? There is a downside—it's so windy in the Galar region, you never really know where you're going to end up!

Meowth-shaped hot-air balloon

FASHION ADVICE

What to wear in the Galar region? Why, disguises of course—especially if you are up to no good, like Team Rocket! In Wyndon, a fetching sunhat and shades helps you to blend in with the tourists. When spying on a secret base, like at Macro Cosmos, try a stylish high-viz top and orange helmet, so you look like a worker!

DON'T MISS:
WOBBUFFET'S GALAR REGION HIGHLIGHTS

- The life of a Team Rocket Pokémon like Wobbuffet is full of **adventure**!

- The Pokémon enjoyed looking **cool in a pink T-shirt** disguise when Team Rocket visited Wyndon Stadium.

- Wobbuffet mastered **vital spy-work**, spotting Pikachu from the balloon, through Team Rocket binoculars.

- It joined the rest of Team Rocket in **blasting off again**.

DOS & DON'TS
WITH . . . TEAM ROCKET'S MEOWTH

Do speak to Meowth. It is one of the only Pokémon who can talk like a human.

Don't doubt Meowth's loyalty to the team. They may argue but Team Rocket are a close crew.

Do ask Meowth for technical advice. It's very smart and resourceful.

Don't go against Team Rocket boss Giovanni. Meowth always tries to follow the boss's orders— he does sign the Team Rocket paychecks, after all!

Torom Island

Scalchop Island

Wayfarer Island

Pinkan Island

ISLAND ADVENTURES

Cave Island

Paladin Island

The Pokémon world has many islands to explore, from small isles with sleepy towns to uninhabited wildernesses, where the only living creatures you will see are wild Pokémon. Many islands are connected to the main regions by ferry or by bridge, while others are remote and only accessible by airplane, airship, or boat. Let's explore!

DECOLORE ISLANDS

This group of lush islands is located off the coast of the Unova region. There are more than twelve islands, each with their own unique sights, tasty foods, and native Pokémon to see. It's not just popular with tropical travelers, but with visiting pirates, too!

Lights Out!
Torom Island is full of hungry Rotom Pokémon. They snack all day on electricity, causing regular blackouts on the island.

What to Pack

Binoculars—For Pokémon watching on Wayfarer Island. It is a well-known rest stop for migrating Pokémon.

A big appetite—For the Grand Harvest Festival held on Harvest Island.

Your own Oshawott or Dewott—To compete in the Scalchop King Competition on Scalchop Island. The contest is a celebration of the shell weapon.

TOP 3 MUST SEES

1. **Honey Island**
   This is the perfect island to visit if you have a sweet tooth! Try the honey made by local Combee and other delicious island desserts.

2. **Cave Island**
   This island has a giant cave with lots of unusual wild Pokémon.

3. **Grand Spectrala Island**
   When the tide is low, take a relaxing walk across the sand from the island to the spectacular Grand Spectrala Islet.

SPOT THAT POKÉMON!

The Decolore Islands are full of new Pokémon to discover! Maybe you'll find Dewott and Oshawott on Scalchop Island, or have an alien encounter with Beheeyem on Capacia Island.

Dewott

Combee

Oshawott

Caterpie

Beheeyam

DOS & DONT'S
WITH . . . ABOMASNOW

Do watch out for the Abomasnow on Paladin Island! It belongs to Morana who is trying to take over Striaton Gym.

Don't let the Abomasnow shake its body. It can cause a terrible blizzard!

Do avoid this strong Pokémon's huge arms! Abomasnow can swing its arms like hammers.

Don't forget that in battle, Ice-type Pokémon are weak against Fire-type Pokémon.

ORANGE ISLANDS

The Orange Archipelago is a large cluster of tropical islands located south of the Kanto and Johto regions. The islands are popular with tourists, who are attracted by the tropical climate and unique sites. Pokémon Trainers also travel here to take part in the Orange League.

TOP 3 MUST SEES

1. Moro Island
This sunny island is home to the popular Moro Island Museum of Art, full of artifacts and artworks. It also has a 300-year-old shipwreck on the coast, said to be haunted by Ghost-type Pokémon.

2. Mandarin Island South
On this large island, Pokémon Master Prima gives lectures and battle demonstrations at her large house.

3. Sunburst Island
The Crystal Caves on this island are home to the rare Crystal Onix, whose body is made from glass crystal.

What to Pack

Your camera—To take photos at the world's first Pokémon theme park, Pokémon Park, on Tangelo Island.

Cat ears and whiskers—To wear while waiting for the arrival of the legendary "Meowth of Bounty" on Golden Island.

Your appetite—For sampling the large grapefruit that grow on the Seven Grapefruit Islands. Watch out for greedy Snorlax, who wants them all for itself.

Snorlax

SPOT THAT POKÉMON

Murcott Island is known for being home to many Bug-type Pokémon. If you trek through the dense forest you can spot Scyther, Venomoth, Paras, and more.

Paras

Top Tip!

Lapras can be a great way to travel from island to island.

Venomoth

Scyther

DID YOU KNOW?

Professor Ivy lives on Valencia Island. She has a huge laboratory to study Pokémon with unusual coloration that appear on the island, such as Nidoran.

NEED TO KNOW: PINKAN ISLAND

- On Pinkan Island, a **special berry** turns Pokémon like Caterpie and Rhyhorn a pink color.

- These pink Pokémon are highly sought after, and **attract poachers** to the island. Because of this, the island's **location is kept secret**.

- Pinkan Island is a **Pokémon Reserve**. Anyone found there (other than rangers, researchers, or Officer Jenny) is questioned.

TRAINER TIPS

- The main Pokémon contest of the Orange Archipelago is called the Orange League.

- Start at the popular tourist destination of Tangelo Island, then fight your first battle at Mikan Island to win the Coral-Eye Badge.

- Next, travel to Navel Island for the Sea Ruby Badge, Trovita Island for the Spike Shell Badge, and Kumquat Island for the Jade Star Badge.

- Now you can enter the Championship in the grand Pummelo Stadium on Pummelo Island to win the Winner's Trophy!

WELCOME TO THE PALDEA REGION

Visit vast lakes, perilous mountains, bustling marketplaces, and farming villages in the Paldea region—the latest region to be discovered in the Pokémon world. There are lots of exciting Pokémon to meet here, from powerful Legendary Pokémon to intriguing new Pokémon friends.

Quaxly

Type: Water

Height: 1 ft 8 in (0.5 m)

This Pokémon likes to keep tidy. Quaxly's feathers secrete a gel that repels water and grime. It also uses a rich cream to slick back the coif on its head and stop it from becoming messy.

Koraidon

This Pokémon is full of mystery. Koraidon can change its form. It can adapt its body to suit the terrain it is traveling over—whether that is on land, water, or through the air!

Miraidon

The mysterious Legendary Pokémon Miraidon, like Koraidon, is said to have powers that far surpass those of other Pokémon. Miraidon can change its form to suit what it is doing.

Sprigatito

Type: Grass

Height: 1 ft 4 in (0.4 m)

Sprigatito is the attention-seeking Grass Cat Pokémon. Its fluffy fur is made from a similar composition to plants, meaning it can create energy by absorbing sunlight.

Fuecoco

Type: Fire

Height: 1 ft 4 in (0.4 m)

This Pokémon loves to eat! It will sprint toward any food it can find. When Fuecoco gets excited, its head spouts more flames.

INDEX

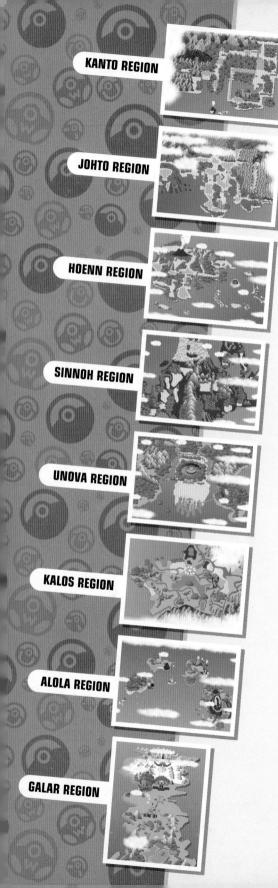

KANTO REGION

JOHTO REGION

HOENN REGION

SINNOH REGION

UNOVA REGION

KALOS REGION

ALOLA REGION

GALAR REGION

Editor Nicole Reynolds
Designers Thelma-Jane Robb, James McKeag
Senior Production Editor Jennifer Murray
Senior Production Controller Lloyd Robertson
Managing Editor Paula Regan
Managing Art Editor Jo Connor
Publishing Director Mark Searle

This American Edition, 2023
Published in the United States by DK Publishing
1745 Broadway, 20th Floor, New York, NY 10019

Page design copyright © 2023 Dorling Kindersley Limited
DK, a Division of Penguin Random House LLC
22 23 24 25 26   10 9 8 7 6 5 4 3 2 1
001–333023–March/2023

A catalog record for this book
is available from the Library of Congress.
ISBN 978-0-7440-6955-6

DK books are available at special discounts when
purchased in bulk for sales promotions, premiums,
fund-raising, or educational use. For details, contact:
DK Publishing Special Markets, 1745 Broadway,
20th Floor, New York, NY 10019
SpecialSales@dk.com

DK would like to thank Hank Woon and the rest of the team at
The Pokémon Company International. Thanks also to Lisa Stock
and Elizabeth Cook for editorial assistance and Julia March for
proofreading and indexing.

Printed and bound in China

For the curious
www.dk.com

MIX
Paper | Supporting
responsible forestry
FSC™ C018179